THE WORLD OF THE
IRISH HORSE

THE WORLD OF THE
IRISH HORSE

GRANIA WILLIS
PHOTOGRAPHS BY JOHN MORRIS

WEIDENFELD AND NICOLSON

LONDON

THE AUTHOR, PHOTOGRAPHER AND PUBLISHERS ARE
GRATEFUL TO CRAIG McKINNEY, CHAIRMAN AND
MANAGING DIRECTOR OF WOODCHESTER INVESTMENTS P.L.C.,
FOR HIS GENEROUS SUPPORT.

First published in 1992 by
George Weidenfeld & Nicolson Ltd
91 Clapham High Street
London SW4 7TA

British Library Cataloguing-in-Publication Data
A catalogue record for this book is available from the British Library.

ISBN 0-297-83052-X

Designed by Andrew Shoolbred

Phototypeset by Keyspools Ltd, Golborne, Lancs
Printed and Bound in Italy

HALF-TITLE PAGE
*Hunter judges Hugh Dunlop and Gina Galvin discuss the attributes of one of the
exhibits, stripped ready for the trot-up, at the Cork Summer Show.*

TITLE PAGE
*Annemarie Crowley, one of Ireland's leading women jockeys, rides Duntree first past
the post at Punchestown. The horse was owned, bred and trained by her father Joe,
but Annemarie took over the licence in 1991.*

CONTENTS PAGE
*A real-life statue? The building blocks of the Irish horse industry are founded on
stamina, courage and tractability.*

ACKNOWLEDGEMENTS

The author and photographer would like to thank the following
individuals and organisations:

Bord Fáilte (Irish Tourist Board)
Ned Campion (SJAI)
Celtic Helicopters
Glandore Clothing Company Ltd
Norma Henderson (SJAI)
Staff of *The Irish Field*
Mary Kelleher (RDS Librarian)
Kodak (Ireland) Ltd
Tony McClafferty
Tony Power
Ada Matheson (IHTS)
Quirke Lynch Colour Laboratory

CONTENTS

INTRODUCTION

IRELAND'S CLAIM TO BE the land of the horse is no unsubstantiated boast. It is an undeniable fact. Ireland simply is the best place in the world to breed horses. Generations of Irish bloodstock breeders have always held this to be the case. But the new money in racing from the multi-millionaire Arabs is now being reinvested in studs in Ireland because it is widely accepted that youngstock raised in Ireland will have an edge over their rivals on the track.

The wild Irish countryside may not look as valuable as the rolling acres of Kentucky's bluegrass country, but the Irish soil contains limestone which produces the depth of bone that marks out the Irish-bred and -raised horse from his foreign counterparts. The mild climate and high rainfall also provide an abundance of grass which the growing youngstock thrive on.

Dermot Weld, who promotes Ireland and the Irish horse through his two training establishments on the Curragh and through his links with the Racing Board, is adamant that Ireland is unique in the world for producing top-class horses. 'We have the limestone soil that they just don't have in England or even in the bluegrass of Kentucky. That's why the

Arabs are all basing their stud farms here and the Aga Khan breeds horses here. It is the best land for producing horses in the world.'

Michael Osborne, ex-manager of the Irish National Stud at Tully and now in charge of Sheikh Mohammed's Kildangan Stud just outside Kildare town, holds the same view. 'Horses grow and develop better here than anywhere else in the world. We are recording average growth rates of 5 per cent per month in our youngstock. Sheikh Mohammed could afford to pick anywhere in the world to raise his young horses, but he wants them all in Ireland because it is the best. Horses have figured very prominently in Irish history for 700 years. The Irish have a natural liking for the horse. I've never met an Irishman who doesn't like a foal. The horse transcends all levels of society.'

Michael Osborne's desire to further enhance the reputation of the Irish horse caused quite a stir during a business trip to America. Michael decided to sport one of the sweat shirts he had commissioned for the staff at Tully and the message emblazoned across his chest turned quite a few heads as he strolled through the arrivals hall on his way to the car hire

---

OPPOSITE: The national carriage-driving championships at Birr Castle. ABOVE: A work horse on the Aran Islands.

ABOVE: *Polo at Phoenix Park, Dublin.*

ABOVE RIGHT: *A Connemara pony and bovine companion pictured from the River Shannon.*

desk. But he was still unprepared for the reaction of the two girls who asked him, in reverential tones, was he really the Irish national stud?

Every level of society is represented in the horse-breeding world in Ireland, from the palatial splendour of Kildangan, the Aga Khan's Ballymany Stud and the Vincent O'Brien/Robert Sangster/John Magnier-owned Coolmore and its satellite farms, through the mixed studs which stand both Thorough-bred and Irish Draught stallions, down to the farmer who keeps a single mare for breeding.

The Commission on Horse Breeding in Ireland, set up in 1900 by the Department of Agriculture, was repeatedly informed of the superiority of the Irish-bred over other horses. One expert reported: 'The excellence of the Irish horse is attributable to the comparative purity of the blood, to the natural advantages in respect of climate and soil which the greater part of the country enjoys, to the habits of the people,

their innate love of the horse, and the keen interest they take in his welfare.'

Even in the mid-nineteenth century Irish bloodstock was recognized as superior. In his book, simply entitled *The Horse*, William Youatt wrote in 1843:

The Irish horse seldom has the elegance of the English horse; he is larger headed, more leggy, ragged-hipped, angular, yet with great power in the quarters, much depth beneath the knee, stout and hardy, full of fire and courage, and an excellent leaper. It is not, however, the leaping of the English horse, striding as it were over a low fence, and stretched at his full length over a higher one; it is the proper jump of the deer, beautiful to look at, difficult to sit and, both in height and extent, unequalled by the English horse.

In 1905 William Ridgeway, author of *The Origin and Influence of the Thoroughbred Horse*, was also unstinting in his praise: 'Irish horses are distinguished for their great development of bone, and for their clean, flat, hard legs, free from the spongy softness of bone so characteristic of British horses.'

The unique cross of the Thoroughbred stallion and the Irish Draught mare, sometimes used as the reverse cross with a blood mare covered by a Draught sire (although usually with less predictable success), has produced the Irish hunter, a horse renowned for its depth of bone, its stamina, jumping ability and equable temperament. This is the basis for the top-class showjumpers that have been sought after by foreign buyers for generations. And, with another infusion of the best Irish Thoroughbred blood to produce extra speed, the Irish-bred horse is also the ideal three-day eventer.

Michael Osborne believes that the reputation of the Irish horse as a jumper, both in the showjumping arena and on the National Hunt circuit, has come about because of his agility and athleticism. 'The Irish horse is supremely athletic. Loch an Easpaig, Rockbarton and horses like them were marvellous athletes. The competition were much heavier horses that had been programmed to jump like robots. The Irish animal had more sheer natural ability. They appear to have more guts than the foreign-breds, but that is really just natural talent and ability.'

That ability is what has singled out the Irish horse and made it into one of the country's best-regarded exports. So much so that, during the reign of Queen Elizabeth I, so many

Irish horses had been sold to Scotland and France that an eleven-year ban was put on further exports between 1566 and 1577. Foreign sales of Irish-breds were also forbidden in 1584 and 1602 and again during the reign of James I.

More than 300 years later the export market was still booming and even the threat of the motor car did little to touch it. In the early years of the twentieth century, William Ridgeway noted: 'Every year the demand for Irish hunters becomes greater and their value increases, and no matter what may be the fate of other classes of horses owing to the competition of motor cars, the high-class Irish hunter is not likely to suffer through the rivalry of any mechanical contrivance.'

An American, Mr F. Moss, writing in the *Thoroughbred Record* in 1933, stated his opinion of the Irish horse in no uncertain terms. 'Just one word about Irish horses. No country in the world is better suited than Ireland for breeding and raising horses and no people more intelligent in breeding horses than the Irish.'

This was backed up by American showjumper Debbie Dolan who competed at the Millstreet International horse show in Co. Cork in 1989. Having seen literally hundreds of Irish-bred horses competing at all levels, from three-year-olds jumping on the lunge to international campaigners, she too was quite clear in her mind, 'There is no doubt that Ireland has the best young horses in the world.'

The traditional use of horses for ploughing has largely died out in Ireland with the introduction of modern farming techniques, but the national ploughing championships are still a popular annual fixture.

CHAPTER ONE

BREEDERS AND STUD FARMS

*I*T IS THOUGHT that the earliest recorded horses in Ireland developed from a mixture of the native animals and Andalusian blood that was introduced by the Spanish Armada in the sixteenth century. Although only small, probably around 13 hands, these Irish Hobbies as they were dubbed, were highly prized. They were described as having a fine head and a strong neck, a well-cast body with strong limbs, being sure of foot and nimble in dangerous places, of lively courage and tough in travel. Exported to England in vast numbers, it is said that the Irish Hobby formed the foundation stock of the English Thoroughbred when cross-bred with the Eastern blood of the Byerley Turk, the Godolphin Arabian and the Darley Arabian.

The Byerley Turk was brought to Ireland by the English Captain Byerley, who was serving in the army of the Williamites. During the fighting at the Battle of the Boyne in 1689 the Captain was cut off from his men and was forced to beat a hasty retreat. The two years on Irish grass and feeding had stood his horse in good stead and he completely outdistanced his pursuers, bringing Captain Byerley into Dublin in record time, to give possibly the best testimonial ever recorded to the benefits of Irish grazing.

The Thoroughbred influence also came into play in Ireland during the eighteenth century as racing began to flourish, but the demands of agriculture required a rather more sturdy animal, probably closer to the Irish Draught horse of modern times, which would be versatile enough to do farm work as well as hunting and the odd bit of driving. By the middle of the nineteenth century the Irish Draught was a well-established type. However, it cannot officially be described as a breed, though many breeders dispute this fact, as there are no records of its original bloodlines and foundation stock.

The Department of Agriculture's *Irish Draught Horse Book*, the first volume of which was published in 1918, stated that

OPPOSITE: *Mares and foals at Coolmore Stud in Co. Tipperary.* ABOVE: *Stallion boxes at Coolmore.*

The Clifden Connemara pony show, held in August, attracts visitors from all over the world to see these renowned ponies on display.

the 'first authentic reference to the Irish Draught horse dates from the close of the eighteenth century.' The book goes on to record: 'One of the most valuable characteristics of the Irish Draught horse was its suitability for mating with the Thoroughbred. To this cross we owe the Irish hunter, which has established for Ireland a world-wide reputation.'

While the conformation of the eighteenth-century Irish Draught remains something of a mystery, its appearance was well catalogued by the middle of the nineteenth century when it was described as:

a long low build of animal, rarely exceeding 15.3 or 16 hands high, with strong short clean legs, plenty of bone and substance, short back, strong loins and quarters, the latter however, drooping and inclined to be what is called 'goose rumped', slightly upright shoulders, strong neck and smallish head. They had good straight and level action, without its being extravagant, and could trot, canter and gallop. They were also excellent jumpers and this is generally recognised as being in some measure the result of their having the strong peculiarly formed quarters mentioned above.

Breeders were keen to maintain the quality of these horses and fought strenuously against the introduction of hackney, Clydesdale or Shire blood. The Breeding Commission of 1900 stated that 'the commercial value of Irish horses is, to a large extent, due to a well founded belief in their comparative freedom from any admixture of so called "soft blood",' referring in particular to the proposed introduction of hackney stallions into Ireland.

The commissioners were as high in their praise of Ireland's unique breed of pony, the Connemara, as they had been of their larger counterparts. They described the Connemara as a breed 'that you could get up on and ride off the grass 30 miles across the mountains, they would never tire, without a feed of oats, nor did not know what the taste of oats was.' The Connemara Pony Breeders Society, which was formed in December 1923, listed the characteristics of the breed as hardiness of constitution, staying power, docility, intelligence and soundness. Not surprisingly it has also been exported widely and Connemara breed societies have sprung up all over Europe and even in the United States.

In 1956 the American Pony Society found that the Connemara fulfilled all its needs, being 'a pony of great stamina and versatility, capable of carrying an adult in the hunt field, yet gentle and tractable enough for a young child, fearless as a showjumper, yet suitable and steady as a driving pony'.

The stamina of the Connemara was proved beyond dispute in 1989 when Ard Go Lightly, 13.2 hands high and bred by Margo and Heather Dean at their Ardmulchan Stud in Co. Meath, won the pony section in the 300 kilometre long-distance ride from Vienna to Budapest. The pony division went up to 15 hands and, in the overall category, which was open to animals of all heights, Go Lightly finished third.

Connemaras now command a high price for export and, as in the half-bred horse industry, many of the top mares were sold out of the country during the 1970s and early 1980s. This trend has not as yet been reversed, but awareness of the situation and the approval of EC funding for the west of Ireland have improved matters, giving breeders the opportunity to retain some of their best bloodlines so that the quality of the breeding herd can be maintained.

Three years before the Breeding Commission was set up at the turn of the century the British Government had voted to give the Royal Dublin Society some financial assistance to promote an improvement in horse breeding. At the insistence of Arthur Balfour, then chief secretary of the RDS, the Government put aside the sum of £5,000 for horse and cattle breeding, with £3,200 of this specifically allocated to the horse industry.

The RDS used these funds to offer £200 premiums for Thoroughbred stallions. With the establishment of the stallion register the monies were then allotted to the individual counties, with a figure of between £80 and £140 being set aside for distribution amongst owners of approved mares in the form of nominations to registered Thoroughbred stallions from 1891 onwards. This scheme continued until the end of 1899.

The Department of Agriculture was founded in the following year and the new Department was entrusted with the administration of all public funds for agriculture, with the exception of the £5,000 grant given to the RDS. However, the Department immediately adopted schemes that were

It is still disputed whether the Connemara is indigenous to Ireland or whether the ponies swam ashore from the wrecks of the Spanish Armada. Co. Clare is visible in the background beyond Galway Bay, where at least five ships from the Armada came to grief.

virtually identical to the Society's policies with the result that, two years later in 1902, the RDS passed on all administration of funds to the Department.

The constant use of Thoroughbred sires, which were the only stallions available in most areas until well into the first decade of the new century, resulted in the Department introducing an experimental scheme in 1904. This involved subsidies of £50 per annum for approved Irish Draught and hunter-type stallions. Between 1905 and 1906 12 stallions were approved and offered subsidies and, by the following year, 38 half-breds, including Irish Draught types, had been entered in the Department register.

In 1911 the Development Commission awarded a grant to the Department of Agriculture for the registration of Irish Draught type mares. The resulting inspections, held on a national basis, yielded 264 mares and 18 stallions suitable to be placed in the register.

Although this scheme was abandoned in 1915, the Department rallied to the cause again two years later, appointing a three-man inspection panel. The inspectors were given the brief of reviving the native draught horse of Ireland and, following further inspections, 375 mares and 44 stallions were passed for entry into the first volume of the Irish Draught Horse Book, which was produced in 1918. The inspectors stated that they had adopted 'a good average standard of merit, and were particularly careful to exclude mares showing coarseness or signs of imported cart-horse blood. No well-made mare that could be regarded as a good, useful farm animal of the clean legged draught type was passed over without careful consideration.'

From 1920 onwards it became an offence to stand an unlicensed stallion at stud. All stallions available for public service were inspected and only sound animals were granted licences. The Horse Breeding Act of 1934 stated that the owner of every entire horse, two years old or upwards, must obtain either a licence or a permit authorizing him to keep the horse entire. The permit was issued on the understanding that the horse would not be used for stud purposes.

But there were still problems within the Irish Draught sector. The findings of a commission of inquiry into the horse-breeding industry, set up in 1935, stated that 'many of what are called Irish Draught horses at present are not of the correct type'. It continued:

With the decline in the number of horses on the land, there is a real danger that the foundation stock of Irish Draught mares will disappear. Because of the economics of the business, these mares and their female progeny are being mated with Thoroughbred sires and fewer of them are being mated with Irish Draught sires … if this trend continues unchecked, the stock of Irish Draught mares will dwindle away to vanishing point and the bone and substance of the world famous Irish hunter will be lost.

Connemara ponies are renowned for their hardiness and ability to survive in the toughest conditions. The number of brood mares has dwindled to approximately 500 due to export. The Twelve Pins (or Twelve Bens) are a magnificent backdrop to this pair of ponies in Screebe, Co. Galway.

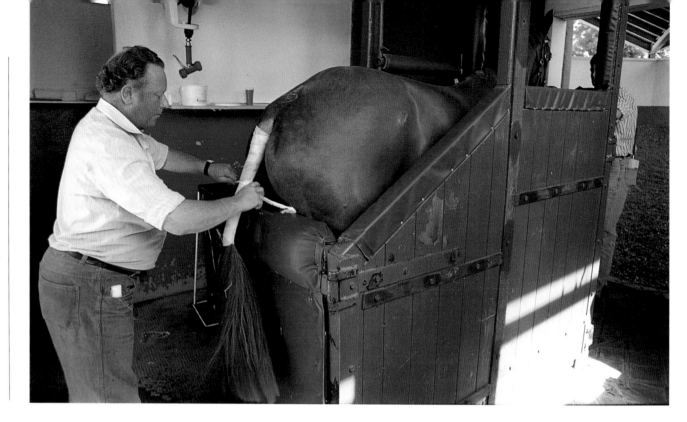

RIGHT: *Preparing a mare for covering by one of the stallions at the Irish National Stud at Tully, Co. Kildare.*

BELOW RIGHT: *Each covering is photographed to satisfy mare owners that the correct stallion has been used at the National Stud.*

BELOW: *Colonel Hall-Walker, the founder of the original stud at Tully before it became the Irish National Stud, was a firm believer in the power of astrology. Six of the original foaling boxes still stand at Tully, showing the high windows which allowed the mares to view the stars prior to foaling.*

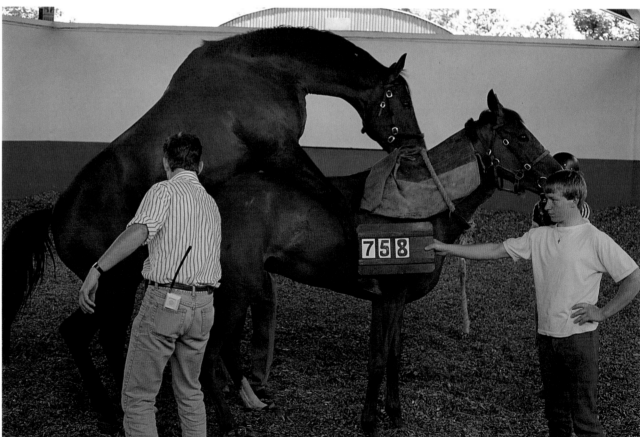

A similar situation in the 1970s brought about the founding of the Irish Draught Horse Society in 1975, hot on the heels of Bord na gCapall (the Irish Horse Board), which had been set up in 1970 through the Horse Industries Act of that year. Bord na gCapall's chief role was the promotion of the non-Thoroughbred horse. The new body took on the responsibility of registering all non-Thoroughbred stock and established the Irish Horse Register in 1974. Education of the people involved in the horse industry also came under the umbrella of this semi-State body, although critics of the Bord say that it spent too much time on educating the people and not enough on stabilizing the breeding of the non-Thoroughbred horse.

Increasing controversy surrounding Bord na gCapall accounts and the registration of stallions resulted in mass resignations in 1982 and the formation of an interim three-man management board made up of civil servants. Several attempts were made to restore public confidence with the appointment of a series of new directors, but criticism of the Bord was by now widespread and it came as no surprise to the industry when it was disbanded in 1987, although its official dissolution did not take place until two years later.

The non-Thoroughbred industry was left in limbo during this period, apart from the announcement by the Minister for Agriculture that substantial funding for the Irish Draught sector would be administered through his Department. The Department also took over responsibility for the Irish Horse Register. But it was not until November 1989, when the Minister announced the nomination of a fourteen-member horse advisory committee, that any attempt was made to fill the void left in the half-bred industry by the disbanding of Bord na gCapall.

Michael Osborne, himself a member of Bord na gCapall for eight years and manager of the Irish National Stud from 1970 to 1982, was openly critical of many of the Bord's policies, claiming that monitoring of the breeding industry was its chief role. Having spent some time in America he now runs Kildangan Stud for Sheikh Mohammed, where as many as 250 two-year-olds will be broken each year before being sent on to their chosen trainers. After the breaking work is done, usually between August and the end of the year, Kildangan then reverts back to its breeding role, with as many as sixty of the Sheikh's mares foaling at the stud before being dispatched to whatever stallion has been selected for them that season.

A Connemara pony teaser at Tully is used to ensure that mares are receptive before the far more valuable Thoroughbred stallions are brought into the covering barn.

Coolmore Stud, the largest
breeding empire in the country,
nestles below the picturesque
Slieve Bloom mountains.

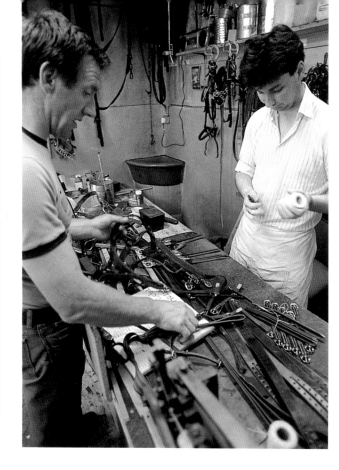

Kildangan had already earned a reputation for producing top-class horses in the hands of former owner Roderick More-O'Ferrall, whose family had bred fifteen Classic winners, in spite of a policy of using the less expensive stallions. Roderick More-O'Ferrall's excellent judgement, after over half a century in the bloodstock breeding world, was proof enough to Sheikh Mohammed that the farm was a perfect site for producing Classic horses. He bought the house, yard and 1,600 acres sight unseen in July 1986. Since then Sheikh Mohammed has added Ragusa Stud at Ballymore Eustace and the Old Connell Stud just outside Newbridge to his Irish holdings. A team of architects has now wrought a complete transformation on Kildangan, all in keeping with the old-style buildings, but with an undeniable opulence that extends to both equine and human inmates.

The Sheikh is not an unseen master, however. To celebrate his 1989 victory in the Irish Derby with Old Vic, the Kildangan staff challenged the Sheikh's English farm, Dalham Hall, to a football match. Kildangan added its own success to the win at the Curragh but, while mere mortals were constantly being substituted on the Naas Rugby Club pitch, Sheikh Mohammed remained on the field throughout and, despite the twin demands on his loyalties, played on the winning side.

Two of the other big names in the Thoroughbred breeding world, Coolmore and the Irish National Stud, have regular battles on the football field. They have other more commercial links, however, such as the sale for £7 million of the National Stud sire Ahonoora to the O'Brien/Sangster/Magnier consortium in 1985. Tragically the stallion was to die while standing at stud in Australia four years later.

The National Stud at Tully, Co. Kildare, only took on the Irish prefix at the end of the Second World War. The stud had been set up at the turn of the century by William Hall-Walker (later to become Lord Wavertree), the owner of the 1896 Aintree Grand National Winner, The Soarer, which he bought for £500.

Hall-Walker had purchased 1,000 acres of prime Kildare land for his new stud, where he was to produce numerous winners. He applied somewhat unconventional methods at the stud, however, using astrology to guide him in his equine breeding programme. A block of six of the original boxes still exists at Tully and each retains the skylight let into the roof through which the eccentric Hall-Walker made his astrological readings before deciding which stallion would cover the mares and when. 'There is no royal road to success in breeding, either by the aid of Astrology, Botany or Physiology, but these all have their use if applied in an intelligent manner,' he wrote in 1908. His unusual methods certainly produced the results and, although the progeny from his first year at Tully won only £770, by 1905 Hall-Walker was at the top of the winning owners' list in England and Ireland, netting himself an impressive £27,400.

Hall-Walker had welcomed a special guest to Tully in the previous year, the 27-year-old Aga Khan, who was fascinated by the breeding techniques used at the stud. Knowing that the Aga Khan was a keen horseman, Hall-Walker recommended that he should take up breeding and racing interests in Ireland. But any plans the young Aga Khan had formed were shelved with the outbreak of the First World War and it was not until the 1930s that he entered into the bloodstock world in Ireland.

The Aga Khan never forgot that it was Lord Wavertree who had planted the idea in his mind of setting up a stud in Ireland and was quick to give him credit for it. 'I would probably never have been known as an owner west of Suez had he not, during and after my visit to Tully in 1904, urged me to take up racing in England. He undoubtedly gave me much good advice, and up to the last I never took an important decision without asking his opinion.'

In 1906 Hall-Walker commissioned a Japanese antiques and art merchant, Tassa Eida, to direct the construction of the Japanese Gardens at Tully. The beautifully laid out gardens depict the seven ages of man, but it was one of the youngest labourers, Eida's son Minoru, who caught Hall-Walker's attention. In honour of the youngster, Minoru, meaning 'light of my eye', was the name given to a colt, bred at Tully, that raced in Edward VII's colours, going on to win the 1909 Derby. The horse came back to stand at Tully for two seasons before being exported to Russia. The Derby winner had a somewhat ignominious end, however, as he disappeared during the Russian Revolution. One of the yards at Tully was also named Minoru, but whether this was to commemorate the horse or the young boy history does not relate.

Since establishing Tully in 1900, Hall-Walker had recorded an impressive list of wins on the Turf. His successes included the Derby, the Oaks, the 2,000 Guineas, the 1,000 Guineas on two occasions, two St Legers, two Ascot Gold Cups and four victories in the Gimcrack Stakes. But in 1915 Hall-Walker decided to present Tully and all its inmates to Britain. The only stipulation was that the Government should purchase the land, at a price fixed by an independent auctioneer. Scrupulously fair in all his dealings, Hall-Walker allowed the British Government to name the auctioneer of its choice.

The property was an extremely valuable one, including as it did the Tully stallions, more than forty top-class brood-mares and the youngstock – all potential winners in the making. Unbelievably, the British Government put off making a decision to accept the gift and, finally, refused the offer, leaving Hall-Walker with no alternative but to instruct Tattersalls to auction the property. After this churlish behaviour, Hall-Walker was gracious in the extreme when he received a telegram from Lord Selborne informing him that there had been a reversal of the original decision. The brief message ran, 'Gladly accept your generous gift of your horses and livestock, buy your properties at Russley and Tully.'

In spite of the fact that the telegram arrived on the eve of the auction, Hall-Walker unhesitatingly cancelled the sale. Captain Henry Greer was brought in to value the property and the sum of £65,625 was duly paid over to Hall-Walker. The livestock had been valued at over £75,000, but the stud's founder stuck to his original plan and presented this valuable asset to the British Government.

Tully was then renamed the National Stud and Captain Greer was appointed as its first manager. But, in 1943, in the middle of the Second World War, the British Government decided to base its National Stud in Dorset and the Tully estate was handed over to the Irish Government.

The Irish National Stud, now managed by John Clarke, has a policy of standing top Thoroughbred stallions at a maximum stud fee of £20,000 although most would be considerably cheaper than that. If a stallion is oversubscribed nominations are decided by ballot. It is not a system that meets with universal approval. Once a horse has been retired to stud it is the results achieved by his progeny which are his strongest selling point, not his own career record. If a stallion misses out on the best mares because of a ballot system this will be detrimental to the stallion and the breeder, with both losing out in the long run.

The National Stud also plays an important educational role within the industry, providing training schemes for farriers, saddlers and apprentice jockeys, as well as taking on a young and enthusiastic staff to service the day-to-day needs of a large and active stud farm.

Coolmore Stud in Co. Tipperary is run on more commercial lines, however, and is the flagship for a whole collection of studs which include Castle Hyde, Longfield, Creek View, Prospect, the Kentucky farm Ashford and Grange, the 300-acre stud which stood Cottage, one of the most influential National Hunt stallions of the 1920s and thirties.

Coolmore had once been owned by Tim Vigors, one of the country's top bloodstock agents, who sold the Aga Khan's Derby winner Tulyar to America for the then record price of £250,000. He had taken over the farm from his father in 1960 and built it up into a flourishing stud standing some of Europe's top stallions, including Thatch, Gala Performance and the £1 million horse Rheingold, winner of the Prix de l'Arc de Triomphe.

In 1973 Vincent O'Brien approached Vigors as a potential purchaser of Coolmore. They were already well known to each other. Some twenty years earlier, as a columnist in one of the Irish daily newspapers, Vigors had expressed his doubts about O'Brien's ability to win the Cheltenham Gold Cup with Knock Hard and also declared himself none too impressed with O'Brien's Grand National hope Early Mist. Both horses came up trumps in 1953, a year in which O'Brien also claimed the Irish Derby with Chamier to notch up an impressive treble. Vigors was not slow to admit the error of his ways, however, and was to play an important role in Vincent O'Brien's career, introducing him to Raymond Guest, the American owner of O'Brien's first Derby winner Larkspur (1962) and Sir Ivor, who won at Epsom six years later.

O'Brien bought two-thirds of the Coolmore property and he and Tim Vigors agreed to approach John Magnier, owner of Castle Hyde stud in Fermoy, to run it. The Vernons pools millionaire Robert Sangster came in with the finance and, eventually, Coolmore and Castle Hyde were amalgamated and John Magnier joined Sangster and O'Brien as a partner. Since then the Coolmore group has expanded to cover over 2,500 acres in Co. Tipperary and has become one of the best known and most successful studs in the world.

Coolmore itself is based on 1,700 acres of prime land just outside Fethard in beautiful Co. Tipperary. Of the thirty-one stallions in the group, twelve stand at Coolmore and all can claim their share of Classic winners. The stallions are all syndicated and Coolmore effectively runs as a stallion broker, selling the nominations to these valuable sires. The shareholders each get a free nomination which they can either use for their own mares or sell. Coolmore sells further nominations to cover the overheads of such an enormous operation and the profits are then divided up amongst the shareholders.

The 600 boxes at Coolmore are split up into eighteen yards, a mixture of old-fashioned loose boxes and American-style barns. Each yard is run independently, with the stallion always being housed in the barn with his mares. This reduces the amount of movement around the farm and also cuts down on the risk of infection.

Top National Hunt sire Deep Run covered well in excess of 200 mares per year during his time at Coolmore, but the more expensive flat stallions are limited to just sixty in a season. Bob Lanigan, general manager at Coolmore, explains that although the figures seem high, the stallions are in fact undertaking the same work load as their predecessors. The improved scientific techniques have resulted in a better understanding of fertility and this in turn means that Coolmore averages less than two coverings per mare.

The number of mares covered also gives a stallion a better chance to establish himself through producing winning progeny. 'A stallion who is restricted to about thirty mares will probably only get twenty runners in his first season. You've got to get about sixty mares to give the horse a chance to get runners, otherwise he won't get winners.'

It is a philosophy that has worked at Coolmore and the other associated studs. But the stallions' work is not necessarily over at the end of the Irish covering season. For some there are more mares to be covered in the southern hemisphere and it was while standing at stud in Australia that Ahonoora died in 1989.

Although Ireland is overflowing with studs (there were close to 850 listed in *The Irish Field* stud directory for 1990), the vast majority cannot compete with the luxury of Coolmore, Ballymany and Kildangan. But there are literally hundreds of small stud farms which stand quality stallions at rather less than the astronomical fees that the top studs can command. Many of these aim to attract mares from all walks of life and, to meet the demand, stand stallions of varied breeding.

Tim Carey's Tullaghansleek Stud in Co. Westmeath, established in 1867, is one of the most cosmopolitan, standing four stallions all of totally different breeding. The 120-acre farm houses the Thoroughbred Euphemism (by Henbit), who is mainly attracting National Hunt mares, the half-bred Golden Cliff (by Blue Cliff) and the Irish Draught Ireland's Pride (by King of Diamonds), both of which were bred at Tullaghansleek, as well as the Connemara pony Silver Cloud, who doubles up stallion duties with teasing mares for his larger stable companions. Prices are competitive at Tullaghansleek: in 1990 Euphemism commanded the highest fee at £300 for National Hunt mares and £150 for half-breds, while both Golden Cliff and Ireland's Pride stood at £100.

Probably the most famous inmate of the Co. Westmeath stud was Blue Cliff, by Preciptic, who became one of the top sires in the showing world and still holds the record for the number of Dublin prize-winners sired. Foaled in 1955, Blue Cliff came to Tullaghansleek as a four-year-old and stood at stud there for a quarter of a century, finally dying three days before his twenty-ninth birthday. But he has left a worthy representative behind him in the half-bred Golden Cliff.

Merrion, one of the country's most important Irish Draught sires and a former Dublin champion, also stood at Tullaghansleek. But the Irish Draught sire that has arguably had the greatest influence on breeding in Ireland is the Slyguff Stud stallion, King of Diamonds. He was bred by Tom O'Neill, who also bred his dam and the sire of his dam, the half-bred True Boy, who goes back to Kildare, one of the most prolific sires at the beginning of this century. The King was produced on the showjumping circuit by John Hutchinson and proved to have spectacular jumping ability, a trait that he passed on to all his progeny. He was retired from active service in 1987 and died at the Bagenalstown stud, Co. Carlow, in 1990.

The reverse cross, using an Irish Draught sire on a Thoroughbred mare, has not proved either as popular or as successful as the traditional mix. This is probably because the

top Thoroughbred mares would normally be bred back to blood sires and not be sent to a Draught stallion. Nevertheless, some good stock has been produced from these matings, most notably in recent years the King of Diamonds mare Mill Pearl who has become one of the top performers on the American showjumping circuit in the hands of the 1984 Olympic champion Joe Fargis.

But is this yet another example of the best horses being creamed off, leaving Ireland to try and breed world beaters from a mare herd that is continually being eroded? Many experts believe that the virtual disappearance of the old-fashioned Irish Draught mare through export is the death knell of the half-bred breeding industry. Others claim that the constant infusion of Thoroughbred blood is also damaging the breed, mirroring the fears expressed by the 1935 commission.

Eileen Parkhill, one of the country's stoutest defenders of the Irish Draught horse and a former member of Bord na gCapall, believes that the traditional habit of continuously going back to the Thoroughbred stallion will eventually produce an animal that is indistinguishable from the Thoroughbred itself. 'The Irish Draught horse has one major advantage over the Thoroughbred in its ability to reproduce its own type. If you start off with a good, well-made Irish Draught mare you are likely to get well-made offspring. The Thoroughbred on the other hand is well known to be a most unpredictable breeder, full brothers and sisters often varying greatly in size and strength, and of course ability.'

Her opinions are in direct contrast to those of Michael Osborne. He states categorically that the dominant genes of the Thoroughbred produce a consistent level of excellence. 'The Thoroughbred is consistent in what it produces, the non-Thoroughbred is not. You can increase the odds of getting what you want enormously by breeding pure bloodlines. The crossing of the Irish Draught mare with the Thoroughbred sire is a magical mixture. It provides the speed, class and stamina of the Thoroughbred with the jumping ability, bone, size and height of the Draught horse.'

The export market is an attractive proposition, however, and how many owners of top Irish Draught mares can afford to turn down a good price for the mare herself or her progeny, no matter how highly prized? Although the Irish Draught is undoubtedly the foundation of so many of Ireland's performance horses, the modern trend is undoubtedly towards a more quality horse. Foreign buyers are now looking for a higher proportion of Thoroughbred blood in the competition horse and the vast over-production in the bloodstock breeding industry could provide the answer.

The Irish Thoroughbred Breeders Association, which was established in 1924 to promote and protect the Thoroughbred horse in Ireland, is seeking to call a halt to the rapidly increasing numbers of foals bred in the Thoroughbred sector. In the last five years of the 1980s the number of foals registered with Weatherbys soared from 4,786 to 6,200. This has brought about a glut of foals on the market, resulting in slackened trade.

The serious nature of the problem became particularly apparent at the foal sales in Newmarket in December 1989 when close to 50 per cent of the catalogued foals failed to make their paper nomination. This meant that breeders were not even covering the cost of the stallion fees, let alone recouping any of the other expenses involved in breeding. The ITBA has been seeking to establish a policy whereby breeders can sell off mares whose progeny are failing to make the grade in the exacting world of bloodstock. These mares could have a valuable role to play in the half-bred sector when crossed with a top Irish Draught sire that has a proven track record on the competition circuit.

Robert Griffin, marketing director of Goffs, believes that there is a similar crisis looming in National Hunt breeding. 'The over-production in the flat sector has resulted in a mass exodus into the National Hunt side. The breeders are behaving like Curragh sheep. When one crosses the road they all do. Now they're all covering their sprint-bred mares with National Hunt sires. It's a cross that does not produce guaranteed results and there will be another glut on the market.'

A total of 10,400 Thoroughbred mares were registered with Weatherbys in the 1989 season, nearly twice the numbers in the half-bred mare herd. Obviously some sort of culling will have to be introduced if a serious downturn in the bloodstock market is to be prevented. Over-production means that vendors can afford to be more critical and only the very top bloodstock will realize its value, while the breeders of the vast majority get stung, particularly in a time of recession.

Robert Griffin recalls being told by a top bloodstock breeder that breeding racehorses is like rose gardening. The secateurs have to be wielded ruthlessly, pruning out the suckers and the dead wood. It is not a coincidence that Henry Cecil's rose gardens are almost as well known in Newmarket as his yard full of Classic winners. Breeding is a tough game, both in the Thoroughbred and half-bred industries, but only by remorseless weeding out can the quality of the progeny be maintained and improved. If breeders cannot afford to go to the top stallions because their youngstock are consistently failing to make their reserves in the sales ring, the quality of future progeny will continue to fall.

John Hughes, the country's leading expert on infertility in mares, is a member of both the ITBA council and the board of the National Stud. He is also on the sub-committee examining the problems of over-production. Hughes spent several years working at the University of Kentucky and, on returning to Ireland in 1970, put into practice the techniques he learnt there while working with most of the top farms in America, such as Claiborne, Gainesway and Spendthrift.

The use of these techniques revolutionized the achievements of an already flourishing group of Irish farms owned by Captain Tim Rogers, who was to die of leukaemia in 1983 at the age of sixty-two. Known throughout the bloodstock industry for his tough no-nonsense attitude, Tim Rogers nevertheless earned the respect of his staff. The Captain's stud groom, Tommy Thompson, now manager at Airlie Stud for Captain Rogers' widow Sonia, declares that Rogers' success within the industry was due to his belief in looking after the small breeder, 'But his idea of a small breeder was a little Jap with £10 million to spend.'

John Hughes credited Rogers with an uncanny ability to pick a stallion. 'He put Ireland on the breeding map of the world. In fifteen years of working with him there were only about four years when we didn't have the top European stallion at one of the farms. Habitat and Petingo were the top two in Europe in the mid-seventies and Sea Hawk was number four.'

Hughes, whose genius would guarantee him lucrative employment at the top stud farms of the world, has no regrets about returning to Ireland. In spite of all his work with the multi-million-dollar farms in America, Hughes, like so many others, believes that Ireland is uniquely blessed with the qualities it takes to breed the best. 'The professional approach to breeding is better in Ireland than anywhere else in the world. The only consistent thing about mares is their inconsistency and the Irish seem to be able to work within those confines better than anyone else.'

Hughes has applied the vast bank of knowledge acquired in America to his work at Airlie and its associated farms where he records an impressively high level of fertility. 'I would be less than happy if we didn't consistently achieve a fertility rate of 85 per cent,' he said. The average in the half-bred sector, where lack of funding precludes the application of such exacting standards, is as low as 56 per cent, although the Irish Draught average is fractionally higher.

Infertility is now virtually a thing of the past at Airlie and Hughes has successfully tackled twinning, the second major headache of breeding horses. The repeatability of twinning in the equine is very high, according to Hughes, but his method of dealing with this is simplicity itself. Through the use of an ultrasound scanner he can establish the presence of twins as early as two weeks, before the immature follicles have had a chance to attach themselves to the uterine wall. Most vets will not scan until at least seventeen days, but Hughes maintains this is too late to deal with the problem of twins. Using the scanner to guide him, Hughes manually squeezes one of the follicles, dispersing the fluid filled sac inside the uterus and allowing the remaining follicle to grow to term. He has been using this technique with phenomenal success since the mid-1980s.

Artificial insemination (AI) and embryo transfer (ET) are techniques which are currently being used with increasing success with sport horses, the new term for non-Thoroughbreds. Although ET is unlikely ever to be accepted in the Thoroughbred industry, the rise in venereal diseases in the horse population could force the use of restricted AI onto the bloodstock world.

Hughes believes that the expansion of these techniques is an integral part of the future success of the non-Thoroughbred industry. 'AI and ET are not just indicated, they're absolutely vital in a small country like Ireland where we don't have an abundance of proven sires. We have to make the most of the top-class stallions and performance mares available to us.'

Argentinian vet José Wade pioneered the use of ET in equine breeding in Ireland. His work has now been expanded upon by Co. Down-based Caroline Berry who has successfully applied to the horse much of the knowledge gleaned through the use of AI and ET in cattle.

Working towards an acceptance of these methods in the sport horse sector, John Hughes now stands John Henry, a stallion son of King of Diamonds, at his 80-acre Williamstown Stud just outside Dublin. The showjumping career of this striking chestnut was tragically cut short by a leg injury caused in a helicopter scare at Crossmaglen, where he was based with James Kernan. The damage to the horse's hock was slow to heal but he is now able to serve mares through both natural covering and AI.

In the world of the sport horse Ireland still produces as many top-class showjumpers as her chief rivals, Germany, Holland and France. This is in spite of the fact that Germany has a pool of approximately 50,000 competition horses compared to Ireland's 3,000.

The Irish Thoroughbred also remains a valuable commodity and, apart from horses sold on the home market, the English sales catalogue a large proportion of Irish animals. As many as 65 per cent of horses sold at the Keeneland Highflyer sales in Kentucky are of Irish extraction. There is no room for complacency, however. The competition is strong and breeding techniques must be continually updated to keep pace with the advances made on the Continent where governmental input, particularly in the sport horse sector, is on a grand scale.

There is no future in resting on the laurels of past successes. Ireland undoubtedly has the raw material to breed champions in all spheres. What is required now is a breeding policy which reflects the superior qualities of that raw material, allowing only the supreme examples of conformation and ability to reproduce.

In the modern world the use of scientific techniques is now an undeniable part of the inexact science of breeding horses. The breeder cannot afford to take chances. He must be selective in his choice of stallion and mare, striving to achieve the magical combination that breeds winners.

There will always be the exception to the rule, particularly amongst the non-Thoroughbreds where distinguished parentage is not a guarantee of success and very often the best performers are bred by accident. The judicious use of veterinary research and the application of the most up-to-date methods available can go a long way towards cutting down on the unpredictable nature of the breeding industry. Science and nature must work hand in hand if Ireland is to remain a contender in the battle for the international equine market.

CHAPTER TWO

THE SALES

*E*VERY HORSE IN IRELAND is for sale, providing the price is right. It may not be a universal truth, but that statement refers to just about 99.9 per cent of the equine population of Ireland.

But being a selling nation brings about its own problems. How often in the past have the Irish had to sit and watch while one of its sons (or daughters) wins the Cheltenham Gold Cup or a prestigious international showjumping Grand Prix for a foreign-bred owner or trainer? In the Thoroughbred sector the market is highly organized, with vendors having a choice of two bloodstock sales complexes, Goffs and Tattersalls. In the half-bred world the outlets are rather more varied, from the official sales at Goresbridge in Co. Kilkenny to the fairs which still feature at venues all round the country. The private sale is usually prompted by a winning, or at least a promising performance which encourages potential buyers to seek out the owner and ask if their horse is for sale. It takes a brave man to say no when the cash is produced.

The vast sales complexes are a relatively recent addition to the horse world in Ireland. The horse fairs have always been the traditional place for selling, although their numbers, and indeed the quality of stock on offer, have tended to decrease every year. Ballinasloe in Co. Galway is one of the few surviving fairs and has been kept together by a determined committee. Always staged during the first week in October, it has a reputation that spreads far beyond the coastal limitations of Ireland. There used to be a spring sale on Ballinasloe's famous fair green, but that has long since disappeared. The attempt to run a fair at Galway racecourse also failed to stand the test of time.

Successful buying at Ballinasloe, or indeed any horse fair, depends on an early start. Horses arrive from dawn onwards and the dealers are quick to spot the bargains. However, buying at fairs is a risky business. All kinds of blemishes, stable vices or temperament problems can be temporarily concealed and the unwary can be caught out all too easily. Your bargain of the previous day can turn into a very expensive mistake. *Caveat emptor* is undoubtedly a caution to be heeded.

Ted Walsh, champion amateur jockey during the 1970s, was a regular visitor to the 12 July fair at Cahirmee near Buttevant, while *en route* to the race meeting at Killarney with

OPPOSITE AND ABOVE: Smithfield market in Dublin.

his father in the late 1950s. For most people the one-day fair would turn into a three-day marathon, arriving the day before the fair and not leaving until the day afterwards. Walsh recalls: 'There were literally hundreds of horses there. A lot of them would be sold to the British army for troopers. But there were no such things as vets in those days. The fellas knew more about horses than the vets did, buying and selling every day of the week. The only thing they couldn't check was the heart, but they did everything else themselves. My uncle Ted used to say that there's no better way to educate you than through your pocket.'

Ted senior had learnt the hard way by buying a cheap horse and proudly showing it to his father when he got it home. His father took one look at it and pronounced that the horse had got a problem. 'But you won't sell him until you meet someone as green as yourself.' The horse turned out to be a shiverer, but was eventually passed on to another innocent. Learning by your mistakes is almost the by-word of the horse fair.

The travellers were past masters at administering weird concoctions which would pacify a vicious or nervous horse. When the unsuspecting buyer discovered the error of his ways, probably the next morning, it would be too late to do anything about it. As if by magic one of the travellers would then appear at the yard, having heard that the farmer was having a bit of trouble with a horse. It would then be bought for half nothing, only to reappear at the next fair, suitably doctored and awaiting its next victim.

But good horses came out of the fairs too. Walsh recalls Ballyrichard, a £125 purchase at Cahirmee on which he won a bumper at Fairyhouse, a maiden hurdle at Tramore, as well as races at Listowel and Leopardstown before it was sold to Anthony and Paul Webber in England where he won eight chases for his new owners. On another occasion a horse that Ted and his father Ruby had taken to Cahirmee to sell attracted no bidders, so they brought it with them to Killarney and Ted won a hurdle race on it.

Many point-to-point horses were also sold at the fair. P. P. Hogan, who was unbeatable in the saddle and remains virtually untouchable now as a trainer of point-to-pointers, was a regular at the big fairs with his father. 'We'd buy fifteen or twenty horses at a time. I remember leading fifteen horses home from Cahirmee once. It was 22 miles. I rode one and led another. The others all had knots tied in their tails and the headcollar rope of the one behind was tied onto that. I was probably riding bareback at about 5 miles an hour. You couldn't do anything but walk.'

To show that a horse had been sold, a halter was put onto it to prevent anyone else bidding for it. These halters were provided, usually at exorbitant prices, by the halter man who was always on hand if a deal was nearing completion. He

Tack is not necessarily a prerequisite for showing off horses at Ballinasloe in Co. Galway. A piece of rope through the horse's mouth takes the place of a more conventional bridle and the rider stays aboard by the seat of his pants and natural balance.

wore a row of cheap webbing halters on his arm ready to dispense one the moment it was needed.

As the haggling reached its conclusion, often after several partings of the ways, during which time a middleman would jump in and persuade the pair to continue their negotiations, hands would be spat upon and then slapped to signify that a price had been fixed. The question of luck money would then arise. A seemingly substantial price can be reduced quite considerably with a favourable luck penny. This sum can vary from literally a penny, which is not unknown, to several hundred pounds, depending both on the generosity of the vendor and the sale price originally agreed upon. Luck money is still an important part of buying horses in Ireland and the seller must always be prepared to part with some of his profit, the more calculating ones taking that into acount when striking the asking price.

The other big fair, which ranked with Ballinasloe and Cahirmee, was the Puck Fair in Killorglin about 6 miles east of Glenbeigh in Co. Kerry. This three-day fair in mid-August is thought to have originated as a pagan harvest festival. However, popular belief holds that the fair is in honour of the wild goats which ran into the village streets to warn the locals that Cromwell's army was on its way, giving them time to defend themselves against the invasion. Whichever theory is the correct one, goats still play a large part in the fair as a wild one is brought down from the mountains and enthroned as King Puck in the village square, its horns adorned with ribbons for the occasion.

Tullow Fair was always held at the beginning of September and it was not unusual to find good point-to-pointers there in the early days. The fair started at the beginning of the Second World War. When war broke out the dealers were left stranded between Tullow and Fermoy with literally hundreds of horses on their way to the boat for England. Rather than return home with these unwanted extras, the dealers congregated on the Tullow road and started selling them. The fair then became an annual event.

Co. Cork was particularly well endowed with fairs. Skibbereen, Roscarbery, Bandon, Drimoleague, Kanturk and Millstreet all held fairs, as did Dunmanway during Dublin Horse Show week at the beginning of August.

Spancilhill was officially held on Midsummer's Day, but it would start at around midnight on Midsummer's Eve and continue for the whole week. Kilrush and Limerick both held fairs four times a year, Limerick's fixtures being staged on the Tuesday before the last Friday in January, April, July and October. Westport in Co. Mayo held a pony fair and foal fairs were run at Clarecastle near Ennis, Kilkea and Newmarket in north Cork. But most of these fairs are now no more.

Ballinasloe, where horse dealing reputedly dates back to the fifth century, is still thriving however. Lord Clancarty, the local landlord, obtained a charter to hold an annual livestock fair in the early years of the eighteenth century, a fair which his family were to develop over the years. The week-long fair reached its peak in the middle of the nineteenth century when an estimated 4,000 horses were sold every year. At that stage sheep and cattle were even bigger trade than horses and, in 1866, it was recorded that 95,000 sheep were sold, with commission of $1\frac{1}{2}$d, and 20,000 cattle, with 6d a head commission.

The mart has now taken over the selling of cattle and sheep, but the horses are still sold on the fair green. Both Ballinasloe and Churchtown in Co. Cork lay claim to having sold Marengo, Napoleon's charger at the Battle of Waterloo. But it is well known that large numbers of Napoleon's chargers were bought at the Co. Galway fair.

An English journalist from the *New Sporting Magazine*, who put only his initials J.R.B. on his copy, recorded for posterity his opinions of Ballinasloe during fair week after a visit in 1834, stating that all the sporting world should make a point of going there.

Confess your ignorance and you are worse than a preacher unequated with the locality of Jerusalem. To be in Erin's green isle when the fair is on and not to be there is a crying sin in the 19th century.

J.R.B. was obviously much impressed with the size of the fair, even before he had got to the green:

Such prancing, dancing, baying, kicking, plunging, jostling, jumping, neighing, spurring I never saw nor heard and, when I got to the fair green, horses, horses again, here, there, everywhere as if all that noble race were crowded together all from the time of Bucephalus to the present time.

If you buy your horse at Ballinasloe you can get all the tack to kit him out as well.

The trotters are paraded Ben Hur style, at breakneck speed, along the newly opened trotting lane at Ballinasloe. Before this was built the trotters were just pointed at the crowd and woe betide anyone who did not get out of the way in time.

It is thought that the learned scribe found accommodation at Corbet's Hotel, in the main street of Ballinasloe, where Wolfe Tone, the founder of Irish republicanism, is reputed to have stayed in 1794. Here, J.R.B. discovered the social delights of Ballinasloe after a hard day on the green:

Mine was a late exit from the ordinary that night and a pleasant jovial night it was. Great challenging, not of gentlemen, but horses. And when I left the room there were many present who could with difficulty tell a horse from …. But no matter, let all be passed over. And oh, that morning I awoke and my head, such a head and such a headache that I had! Ring, ding, ding go the bell. Soda water, and be quick! Confoundedly bad wine it must have been that I drank last night. It was not till after I had seen my

bill, the worst I had ever met at any hotel, that a full sense of my previous night's exploits came before me. For, beside wine, there was more brandy charged to me than I drank for a month before – much more, I inwardly vowed, than I would drink for the next six!

Shortly after J.R.B.'s dissertation on the delights and otherwise of Ballinasloe, a serious crisis is said to have arisen in the Cork distillery which regularly provided the whiskey for consumption during fair week. In 1847 it was reported that the distillers were extremely distressed to note that a mere eight gallons of whiskey had been sold, a positive trickle compared to the 800 gallons consumed two years previously. Father Mathew, in whose honour the Aintree Grand National winner of that year had been named, had obviously found rather too many subscribers to his oath of abstinence for the whiskey producers' liking!

Father Mathew's influence has long since waned and the publicans of the Co. Galway town certainly have no cause for complaint in modern times, even though their premises and the staff that man them are unlikely to get any sort of a break during the week-long proceedings.

Possibly the best known horse to have been sold at Ballinasloe in recent times is Leapy Lad, which was jumped on the Aga Khan team at Dublin by George Stewart before being exported to America for £250,000. Leapy Lad changed hands at Ballinasloe as a three-year-old. Now ridden by Jay Land he has become one of the top Grand Prix horses on the tough American showjumping circuit.

The horse-of-the-fair showing classes were introduced in an attempt to improve the quality of horses at Ballinasloe. Technically speaking horses must be for sale to be eligible for these classes. However, the top showing stables frequently use Ballinasloe either as a wind-up to the current season or to test the water before their raids on the major fixtures the following year, and it is unlikely that the owners of these valuable creatures are open to offers.

Ballinasloe during horse fair week is milling with all things equine. Even the roads into town are crammed with horses that have not managed to get as far as the green. Wall-eyed foals trot in-between the stationary cars, blissfully ignorant of the scarcely concealed rage of the vehicle's occupant after several hours of inching his way towards his Mecca, the fair green itself.

There are still some quality animals to be found once you attain your goal, but an experienced eye is needed. The fair green now has a railed-off lungeing and jumping area. In previous years partly broken horses were flung at makeshift fences by their enthusiastic, if not totally orthodox, jockeys. Spectators were constantly in danger of being mown down, although surprisingly there never seemed to be any serious accidents as hopeful vendors reeled-in explosive three-year-olds on the end of tangled lunge lines.

There are two distinct areas of the fair, although the only demarcation line is the change from grass to concrete. The more quality hunters and potential showjumpers are to be found on the green itself, while the coloured cobs and working horses mill around on the concrete, mingling with the chip vans and cardsharps.

A new trotting lane backs onto the lungeing area and it is on this that the lads now demonstrate their mounts' speed, usually bareback with their feet thrust forward to absorb the jarring gait as the cobs beneath them hammer up and down the concrete strip. This hazardous occupation is now relatively tame compared to the old days when the lads would

simply charge straight at the crowds, scattering people to left and right in their wake.

Smithfield market in Dublin is not dissimilar, except that the cobbled square offers even less grip for roughly or even unshod hooves as their owners clatter and slide their way across the surface while being put through their paces for possible buyers. Smithfield is right in the heart of Dublin, but on the less fashionable north side. It is a fruit and vegetable market for most of the year, becoming a horse fair only on the first Sunday of every month.

By midday the square is swarming with people, horses and ponies, the occasional donkey, sulkies, traps, vans selling second-hand harness and tack, not to mention the enormous lorries used to transport the horses. The market attracts more

of the same coloured horses and ponies that appear at Ballinasloe, but the odds against discovering a potential Grand Prix showjumper would make any respectable bookie blanch. The odd pony will be plaited and well turned out, but most are left very much to nature. It does not seem to put the buyers off, however, and there is no shortage of interested parties for all types.

Dromore horse fair in Co. Down also has its share of cobs and ponies of varying colours. But, like Ballinasloe, it also holds showing classes, so that customers get a good chance to view their prospective purchases and take in the opinion of the judges, before terms are discussed. The main road through the town is sectioned off into rings. The heavy horses take over one of these, while the youngstock and broodmares are

Smithfield marketplace in the centre of Dublin turns into a horse fair on the first Sunday in every month. Whatever your requirements, the dealers will do their best to persuade you that their horse is perfect for the job.

LEFT: *The fair green at Ballinasloe is a mass of humans and equines during the October horse fair.*

ABOVE: *The halter man was a familiar sight at the horse fairs around Ireland and would sell cheap webbing halters for buyers to lead their purchases home. This upmarket halter man was seen at Goffs.*

35

minutely examined in another by judges squeezed into their Sunday-best suits, with a bowler precariously perched on the head to complete the effect.

Spectators pack round the makeshift barricades, keenly awaiting the judges' decision, which is more often than not met with hoots of derision from the ringside adjudicators who are convinced that the horse in second place should have won. A blacksmith demonstrates his craft to another audience, while the children clamour for candy-floss and other sticky delights from the stalls that share the pavements with tack shops and barrows heaped with junk.

A door midway down the street offers enticement to the crowds now beginning to throng the town: 'Thru' this way for home-made soup and stew. £1, including bread.' The gloomy passageway that is revealed through the half-open door does not seem to be thick with clients, shades of Sweeney Todd apparently keeping all but the most desperate out.

But the half-bred industry does have official outlets. Bord na gCapall set up sales at Gowran Park racecourse in 1974 with the aim of attracting foreign buyers back to Ireland. The gap left when the Bord sales were discontinued has now been filled by the Donohue family's Goresbridge complex which holds monthly fixtures as well as special extended sales for showjumpers and eventers.

Thoroughbreds are catered for by Goffs in Kill, Co. Kildare and the new sales complex at Fairyhouse which is run by Tattersalls (Ireland) following the move from Ballsbridge in 1988. The rivalry between the two firms has undoubtedly helped the market, even though the split in 1974 seemed a retrograde step.

The name of Goff had been associated with sales in the world of bloodstock since 1866 when Robert J. Goff announced his appointment as official auctioneer to the Turf Club. Based in Newbridge, Co. Kildare, Goff stated that he was willing 'to attend any race meetings, receiving due notice, to dispose of winners of selling stakes, or conduct sales of bloodstock.'

The following year Robert J. Goff held his first yearling sale in the RDS paddocks at Ballsbridge. The first lot to come under the hammer was a brown filly by Arbitrator who was knocked down to the highest bidder for 330 guineas; a long way from the telephone numbers that now appear on the computerized display units, which reveal the price in Irish punts, pounds sterling and American dollars.

Goffs became a limited company in 1922 under the chairmanship of Edward Kennedy, breeder of the spotted wonder, The Tetrarch, at Straffan in Co. Kildare. The horse was bought as a yearling in 1912 for the monstrous sum of 13,000 guineas by Atty Persse, who in turn sold him on to Major Dermot McCalmont.

Nearly every type of horse and pony can be found at Smithfield. While you may not find a Derby winner or a Grand Prix showjumper, there are plenty of genuine work horses to be had.

The traditional spitting and slapping of hands is still to be seen at the conclusion of deals. The fair green at Ballinasloe is crowded with people keen to assist in the bargaining.

The Tetrarch was unbeaten in his seven races as a two-year-old and was claimed to be the fastest horse in the history of the Turf. But leg problems caused his early retirement to stand at the McCalmont family's Ballylinch Stud at Mount Juliet. During an illustrious stud career The Tetrarch sired Tetratema, winner of the 2,000 Guineas, who in turn sired Mr Jinks, the horse that brought about McCalmont's second 2,000 Guineas success.

The fortunes of Goffs were also in the ascendant. Turnover showed a rapid climb from £19,000 per annum in 1925 to £$\frac{1}{2}$ million by the mid-1950s, with as many as eight Grand National winners passing through the sales ring in that period. Other National Hunt heroes who changed hands at Goffs were the triple Gold Cup winner Golden Miller, who also went on to win the Grand National, the legendary Arkle and the equally revered Red Rum. The ill-fated Devon Loch, who looked set to carry the Queen Mother's colours to victory in the 1956 National, was also sold in the Goffs ring, as was the horse who galloped past Devon Loch's spread-eagled form to win that year, ESB. Two Epsom Derby winners, Hard Ridden and Larkspur, found new owners with the help of Goffs' auctioneers, as well as eight horses that went on to claim the Irish Derby.

But the sale of the RDS bloodstock paddocks in 1973 was to bring about an enormous change in the Thoroughbred market in Ireland. The backwash of the oil crisis had caused a slump in the bloodstock trade and the prospect of holding sales in the pig parlour in the RDS main hall did not appeal to the directors of Goffs, headed by Robert and Philip Myers-cough. A meeting was arranged between the Irish Thoroughbred Breeders Association and the RDS at which direct communication links seemed to break down. The breeders departed having understood the RDS president, Professor James Meenan, to have stated that the RDS would not be building a new sales ring.

The direct result was the erection of a massive complex at Kill in Co. Kildare and Goffs opened for trade in the new premises in August 1975, in spite of a reversal of the RDS decision. This was probably brought about through the realization that Goffs had provided the Society with an income of between £40,000 and £50,000 annually, based on a sliding scale linked to turnover.

The RDS now stated that it would build a sales complex to replace the paddocks which had been sold the previous year. Standish Collen's family building firm, Collen Built, were given the brief to build a dual purpose complex which could alternately be used for stabling 300 horses, holding pop concerts or motor shows. Three generations of the Collen family have been responsible for the building of the entire Royal Dublin Society, right from the time of its move from Leinster House in 1924. More recently the fourth generation

LEFT: *Tattersalls' vice-chairman David Pim encourages buyers to dig deeper in their pockets.*

BELOW: *Ponies are put through their paces, regardless of the hordes that throng Smithfield on market day.*

has been in charge of the structural improvements that have been carried out at the showgrounds.

In response to the news that the RDS would be holding bloodstock sales in direct competition with Goffs, Paddy McGrath put together a syndicate of seven shareholders to finance the project at Kill. McGrath, Mr and Mrs Bertram Firestone, Walter Haefner of Moyglare Stud, Captain Tim Rogers, Dr Schnapka of Ferrans Stud and Fasig Tipton Inc. were later joined by the Aga Khan and Robert Sangster as the major shareholders. The first sale in the new complex was held less than a month after the opening and was, according to the then managing director Jonathan Irwin, 'a tremendous success. It put the whole market back on its feet. There had been such gloom and despondency, but it turned the whole thing around.'

Goffs blossomed in Kill, achieving record prices for foals. A new company was bought in Paris and it was Goffs (France) that was to sell the French and Irish Derby winner Assert to P. P. Hogan on behalf of Robert Sangster for a mere £16,000.

Back in Ballsbridge, meanwhile, the Thoroughbred breeders, headed by Larry Ryan, approached the RDS with a proposal that a joint-venture should be initiated between the two bodies to run a sales company. Ballsbridge Bloodstock Sales, financed mainly by the RDS, achieved a £$\frac{3}{4}$ million turnover that year.

It was agreed, however, that the new company did not have sufficient muscle to provide the breeder with a strong alternative service. Competition is good in any business and the prospect of two top sales outlets in Ireland was the one thing that might work to prevent the continual drain of Irish horses being sold through Newmarket. It was estimated that nearly 60 per cent of the horses that passed through the Tattersalls sales ring in England had originated from Ireland. This led to formal discussions with Tattersalls, with the result that a new company, Ballsbridge Tattersalls, was formed under the chairmanship of Standish Collen. Fifty per cent of the new company was owned by Tattersalls, headed by Co. Donegal-born Michael Watt, while the remaining 50 per cent was held by the RDS and the Thoroughbred breeders. The first sale under the new name was held in June 1979.

It was during the days of Ballsbridge Tattersalls that David Pim, vice-chairman and one of the top auctioneers in the company, was trying to encourage a reluctant bidder to put his hand deeper into his pocket. All auctioneers have their own catchphrases which they fall back on during slack bidding and Pim resorted to his favourite, 'I know you'll like him,' even adding as the final persuader, 'I like him myself'. It did not have quite the required response, however, as Mick O'Toole called out in a stage whisper, 'Well why don't you f...ing buy him yourself then?'

More changes had taken place on the Tattersalls front in

If you cannot get the right car at Smithfield you will at least find horsepower of some sort.

1985 when the RDS and breeders' interests were bought out to form Tattersalls (Ireland) headed by Denis Mahony. It was then decided that the premises at the RDS were less than satisfactory for the increasing demands being made on them by both the bloodstock sales and rival attractions.

Enormous new premises were built opposite Fairyhouse racecourse in Co. Meath at the cost of £5 million. David Pim, who was to mastermind the building of the new complex, states that there was only one item on the architects' drawing that was not revised. That was the octagonal sales ring. 'The stabling plans were altered drastically. There was no point making the same mistake as Goffs. All our stabling uses the barn system so that a horse can be brought from any barn to the parade ring under cover.'

Pim reflects on the day in the mid-1970s when he stood up at the meeting between the ITBA and the RDS to state that the last thing Ireland needed was two sales complexes. 'But it has turned out to be exactly what was needed. The competition is very healthy and has opened up the whole market.'

After its first full year in the new premises, specializing mainly in the National Hunt market, Tattersalls (Ireland) had boosted its 1988 turnover by 23 per cent to 14 million guineas. Goffs, where the chief market is in the much more lucrative flat-bred yearlings, realized 39 million guineas in 1988, but it is the closing of the gap between the two companies that is most remarkable. In 1984, when Goffs achieved a record 40 million guineas, Tattersalls (Ireland) was turning over a mere 4.4 million guineas. It has now cornered the increasingly lucrative National Hunt market and, according to chairman Denis Mahony, is now aiming to stake its claim to a large slice of the flat market as well.

Goffs' 1984 peak was to crash over the next two years, however, the falling market resulting in a 38 per cent drop by 1986. The massive investment in European bloodstock by the Middle East, which had initially boosted trade, brought about a serious decline in the Irish market during the mid-1980s.

Seeking to arrest the move by the Irish breeders back to the traditional nest at Newmarket, Goffs' managing director Jonathan Irwin reworked an idea that had originally been used in Australia in an attempt to revitalize flagging trade. 'The decline was an inadvertent by-product of the massive investment by the Middle Eastern families. They were buying in huge quantities and placing their purchases with the top twenty trainers in Europe with the result that the trainers didn't have to go out and look for new owners,' explains Irwin. 'I would liken the racing industry to an octopus. The breeding industry is its body and the tentacles are the trainers and bloodstock agents who would normally spend twelve months foraging for new business. When the Arabs eliminated the top trainers it was the same as if the tentacles had been cut off the octopus. A formula to break that stranglehold was urgently needed.'

Irwin found exactly that formula in Queensland where Carl Waugh had launched his Magic Million. In spite of the fact that Queensland was the most minor of the breeding states in Australia, the idea of a race that was restricted to horses catalogued at a special sale, appealed to the fickle industry that is racing. The sale expanded to become one of the top four most important yearling sales in the whole of Australia, in a state that had previously never been considered as a contender. If it could work in Australia, it would work in Ireland, reasoned Irwin. The equation of a strictly limited number of horses with a very big pot on offer at the end was bound to capture the imagination. And the pot, in Irwin's mind, had to be £1 million.

Goffs had returned a loss of £450,000 in its 1986 figures. And, less than a year later, here was the company's managing director asking the board to underwrite £1 million. The chances of success seemed slim. But Paddy McGrath gave

OPPOSITE: Goffs, the older of the two bloodstock sales companies in Ireland, still holds the European record for a yearling. A colt by the ill-fated stallion Shergar was sold for 3.1 million guineas at the Co. Kildare sales complex.

LEFT: Former Curragh trainer Kevin Connolly was a regular at the Irish bloodstock sales before his departure for Macau in the middle of 1991.

The concept of The Million sale and its accompanying race, which carried the Cartier banner until 1990, was the brainchild of Jonathan Irwin and was instrumental in the turnround of Goffs' finances.

45

The vendors can often be as young, if not younger, than the horses they are selling. But youth is no guarantee of getting a bargain and is often quite the opposite.

Irwin his support and, eventually, the rest of the board followed suit, with the exception of the Aga Khan who, as an owner/breeder would automatically be excluded from aiming for this particularly juicy plum.

The stewards of the Turf Club, led by Lord Hemphill, gave their approval of the scheme. It was an act of extreme bravado as both the English Jockey Club and its French equivalent sought to have the decision reversed. The Turf Club remained immovable and it was left to Irwin to put the finishing touches to his plan of campaign.

The scene was set. Goffs would hold an exclusive yearling sale in October of that year and, twelve months later, the selected two-year-olds would be eligible to race for £1 million at the Phoenix Park. There was one major drawback, however: no sponsor had been found. Undaunted, Irwin asked the then Fianna Fail leader Charles Haughey to launch The Million in front of 100 guests at a top Dublin hotel.

Due to a clerical error, the banqueting manager, covered in confusion, was forced to reveal the appalling news that there was no room available for the announcement of this prestigious addition to the Irish sales and racing calendar. The bar was the only alternative, so Charles Haughey officially launched The Million in front of the assembled guests, much to the amazement of the tourists who had dropped in for a quiet pint!

The Goffs board of directors made it patently clear to Irwin that there was no budget to promote his brainchild. But, within ten days of contacting a London PR agent, Caroline Neville, the deal with Cartier was sewn up. 'It was the best name I could have got,' said a triumphant Irwin. 'The name changed the whole image.'

Cartier agreed to foot the not inconsiderable bill for promoting both the sale and the race, but did not contribute to the jackpot prize. In effect they were merely loaning their name in order to lend kudos to the whole affair. But it worked and, when the first Cartier Million sale hit the rostrum at Goffs in October 1987, it resulted in a massive turnaround for the company's flagging finances. Its losses of just under £$\frac{1}{2}$ million were suddenly transformed, almost overnight, into a more comfortable bank balance of £400,000.

Even more flattering for Goffs, however, were the carbon copies of the Cartier Million effected by Tattersalls in England, who linked hands with Tiffanys, and the deal signed between Agence France and Piaget, both sparked off by the success of the Irish project.

Irwin believes that that success was brought about because the scheme catered for the buyer who had previously been wiped out by the home-produced horses. 'There are over 70,000 Thoroughbred foals produced in the northern hemisphere every year. If you buy a good horse, the chances are that you run into an even better one racing for its owner/breeder, a horse that your agent has never had the chance to try and buy because it hasn't been offered at a public auction. The Million scheme offered a restricted sale with massive prize-money as the lure at the end of the day. It achieved its aim because it boosted sales tremendously and brought some big names into racing, like Chris de Burgh. I never wanted a Group race, I just wanted to revive the sales figures.'

But the venture was to be dealt three severe body blows, almost before it had got into its stride. Its creator, Jonathan Irwin, severed his links with Goffs in November 1989, less than two months after the second Cartier Million race at the Phoenix Park. A month later Cartier issued a statement declaring that the 1990 Million would be the last to carry the Cartier tag and it was to be that very race that sounded the death knell of the racecourse itself as the Phoenix Park finally closed its gates, with no hope of rising from the ashes as it had seven years earlier after a temporary closure.

The recession that had, in part, brought about the downfall of Dublin's only metropolitan racecourse, also bit hard into the bloodstock market at the beginning of the 1990s. Sales figures in both the Thoroughbred and half-bred sectors plummeted and the record prices of the late eighties were consigned to memory rather than bank balances. Realism was a bitter pill to swallow for many breeders, but the inflated prices had brought about over-production which, in turn, had flooded the marketplace.

Quality will always find a buyer and, as long as the Irish breeder continues to produce the right article there will be an auctioneer to seek the highest bidder. While there are horses in Ireland, there will always be sales, whether it be the rarefied atmosphere of Goffs and Tattersalls, or the hand-slapping deals conducted on the fair green at Ballinasloe or Smithfield.

CHAPTER THREE

THE SHOWS

*H*ORSE SHOWS are such an integral part of the Irish equestrian scene that it is hard to imagine a time when they did not exist. But even the world renowned Dublin Horse Show, now held on the hallowed turf of the Royal Dublin Society during the first week of August, only dates back as far as 1864 and is by no means the oldest show in the country.

Both Piltown in Co. Kilkenny and Ballinasloe in Co. Galway claim to have appeared on the calendar first. The records for Ballinasloe reveal that in 1800 the Farming Society of Ireland resolved to hold shows in Smithfield in Dublin, Limerick and Ballinasloe and that the first show was staged in Ballinasloe on 7 October of the following year.

On display were cattle, sheep, pigs and draught horses, with the top agricultural stock earning the then enormous premiums of £50. There were also ploughing competitions for which the first prize was £10 or a gold medal. In those early days the horticultural section of the show was staged in the town hall, built by Lord Clancarty on Society Street adjoining the fair green. It was the Earl's ancestor who had set up the horse fair in Ballinasloe at the beginning of the

previous century. However, it was not until 1839 that the agricultural, livestock and horticultural sectors of the show were amalgamated and it is this year that is recognized as the official start of the Ballinasloe fixture which celebrated its 150th anniversary in 1989.

The Piltown show also has a chequered history having been started in 1826 by the Earl of Bessborough, a descendant of one of Cromwell's officers, and the possessor of an enormous estate known as the Barony of Iverk, consisting of the combined parishes of Mooncoin and Piltown and pieces of other parishes as well.

The so-called shows of the 1820s took the form of challenges set up by the enlightened Lord Bessborough in an effort to educate and encourage his tenant farmers and estate workers. The Earl arranged contests for the best kept cottage, the best maintained cottage garden and the best half-acre of wheat or turnips. Judges were appointed to adjudicate throughout the season.

Show day itself was an annual holiday on the estate. The Earl of Bessborough was chairman of the show and the gentlemen farmers were charged with the organization. The

OPPOSITE: The trade-turnout class at Dublin Horse Show. ABOVE: The judges' box at the Cork Summer Show.

An aerial view of a mare and foal class being judged at the annual Connemara show at Clifden. This August fixture is frequently hit by wet weather.

entrance fee of one shilling put off most of the less well paid, however. They reasoned that they could buy six pints of beer at 2d a go, far better value than spending the day at the show, unless of course they could get in free. The main job for the ordinary workers was to try and prevent the peasantry from climbing the estate walls in their attempts to get into the show for nothing.

It was not until the mid-nineteenth century that the show was moved to a central venue. There had always been an annual gathering of the tenants and peasantry for the prize-giving, when hats had been doffed and knees bent, but by the beginning of the new century the uprise of national feeling had caused a considerable change in attitude towards landlords and when, in 1920, the then Lord Bessborough made an anti-Sinn Fein speech in the House of Lords, the committee moved the show out of the Iverk estate in protest.

Even a typically 'soft day' cannot wipe the smile off the features of British chef d'équipe Ronnie Massarella as he is presented with the gold-plated Aga Khan trophy by the former president of Ireland, Patrick Hillery, after a British victory in the Nations Cup.

Showjumping had become a regular feature on the programme by the time the first Prime Minister of the Free State, W. T. Cosgrove, attended the show in 1926. A grandstand was erected specially for the occasion; it was stored in the local creamery and reassembled every year.

The Piltown show of 1938 was the last for a decade. In 1948, with the Second World War safely over, an indoor vegetable and flower show was held. It was not until 1951 that any action was taken to restart the equestrian and agricultural side of the programme. Members of the commit-tee met with Mattie Brennan (father of Tommy Brennan), Tom Hughes, Jim Finnegan and Michael Costello.

It is said that the four experts did all the talking while the show committee did all the drinking. Nevertheless a com-pletely new schedule of events was drawn up, including a full jumping programme. Searches of the creamery, however, failed to reveal any remnants of the original grandstand.

RIGHT: *The elegant art of side-saddle riding has all but disappeared in the hunting field, but the two ladies' hunter classes at Dublin (in which exhibits must be ridden side-saddle) always attract a good entry.*

BELOW: *Commandant Gerry Mullins puts the Kerrygold ribbon onto Glendalough's bridle after a win at Dublin, while Joe Moorhead keeps a firm hold on the reins.*

In 1951 the show made takings of 25 shillings from the sole trade stand on display. Profits closer to £8,000 are now the order of the day and the committee has bought the 35-acre site where the show is held on the first Thursday of September.

The historically much older Royal Dublin Society did not stage its first agricultural show until April 1831, 100 years after the RDS itself was founded. Horses formed a very small part of this three-day spring meeting, however. The class for agricultural draught stallions attracted only six entries and there was also a section for donkeys, or, as they were termed then, 'Spanish asses'.

When the horse show was first mooted in 1867 there were no plans to add showjumping to the schedule, but in June of that year Lord St Lawrence (later to become Lord Howth) put forward a proposal: 'this committee ... have come to the conclusion that it would prove expedient to offer prizes for jumping, especially as such a course will be attended with little or no pecuniary risk, and will add considerably to the attraction of the Horse Show.'

At the 1868 show, which was held in the courtyard of Leinster House in Kildare Street (now the home of the Irish Parliament or Dail), there were two jumping competitions, a high leap and a long leap. There was a championship on the final day over a stone wall, described in *The Irish Farmers' Gazette* of the period as '5ft 10in, in cold blood, off wet sawdust, in a crowded courtyard'. A silver cup plus £10 was on offer as inducement to summon up the necessary courage to tackle this awesome obstacle, but horses had to qualify in

earlier heats before being allowed to take part in the championship. The qualifying rounds were held over a mere 4ft 10in, the fence itself being made of three bars on pivots, trimmed with gorse. Presumably the addition of the gorse was for decorative purposes and not designed to discourage the horses from hitting the top rail.

The receipts for the 1868 show were £1,856.9s and, once the total expenditure for the three days had been calculated, the coffers showed a profit of nearly £162. The refreshment stand had not proved as successful as originally hoped, however, making only £5 throughout the show. It is thought that the lack of a temporary licence, which meant no alcoholic beverages, was the cause of this slim profit margin.

The success of the show guaranteed its place in the calendar for the following year. The Kildare Street premises were used again in 1869 and 1870, when the three-day meeting became known as the National Horse Show. But, in both 1871 and 1878 the Royal Agricultural Society of Ireland held its shows 'in a field at Ball's Bridge'.

By 1879 it had been agreed that the RDS and the RASI should join forces and, in that same year, the RDS leased 15 acres of land at Ballsbridge from the Earl of Pembroke, for rent of £180 per annum over the next 500 years. The Society spent £11,690 on building premises on the new site including the removal of the Agricultural Hall, which had been opened

in Kildare Street in 1858, to Ballsbridge where it was renamed the South Hall.

Following a successful Spring Show in 1881 it was agreed that a further £1,000 should be spent on a grandstand in the jumping enclosure. At that stage there were only three obstacles in the enclosure: a double bank, stone wall and water jump.

The jumping classes were already beginning to change. The original guidelines had simply laid down that the obstacles were to be cleared 'to the satisfaction of the judges', although 'superiority of form and style of fencing' became an added criterion. The classes were designed specifically for hunters as there was no question of specialized showjumpers in those early days.

Judging was done on a purely subjective basis and, to add to the problems, Society members claimed the right to enter the judging ring during the classes. This was stopped at a Society meeting convened specially for the purpose in 1873 when a resolution was passed empowering the Horse Show committee to 'clear and keep the ring and jumping and excercising grounds free of all persons whomsoever, whether members of the Society or others.'

The move to Ballsbridge was to bring about several major changes in the programme of events and the way competitions were run. The three fences in the new jumping enclosure were used for the leaping competitions at that first show in 1881, when a minimum weight of 13st was brought in, with four-year-olds being given a 14lb allowance. By the following year a course of jumps had been introduced, including a ditch and bank, a stone wall, hurdle, double bank and water.

Transport problems for both equine and human showgoers were solved by the new RDS railway siding which was opened in April 1893. One northern exhibitor can remember being told by his grandfather that a special train was commissioned to take horses from Ballymena to Ballsbridge. The locals would all flock to the Co. Antrim station to watch around 200 horses being loaded onto the train. The horses travelled on a one-way ticket so they all had to be sold at the show.

Showjumping had rapidly become popular and, following the example of the Ballsbridge enclosure, jumping courses were erected at show grounds all round the country. The competitions were a great diversion for the public and as many as 10,000 would flock to Ballsbridge on each afternoon of the Horse Show.

Entries in the jumping classes had soared and it became necessary to run the horses in pairs, which resulted in even more haphazard judging of the competitions. William Evelyn Wylie, who was to become one of the most respected names within the Society, felt particularly aggrieved about this as,

having made the long trip down from Coleraine, he was twice the victim of apparently indiscriminate judging. He went on record as saying: 'If I ever have sufficient influence or have a say in the affairs of the Royal Dublin Society, my first effort will be to frame some rules.' It was no idle threat and, although it was some time before he could put it into practice, Judge Wylie was to become the man who, almost single-handedly, brought Irish showjumping into the twentieth century.

During the First World War the military authorities commandeered the Ballsbridge premises and the RDS was once again confined to Leinster House. By 1919 the RDS was reinstated in Ballsbridge, but the military had done considerable damage to the site and the financially embarrassed Society had little success in attempting to recoup some of its losses through compensation.

The Horse Show reappeared on the calendar that year and, with jumping classes on the programme every day, made record profits. There was also a new class added to the schedule, for women riders who had previously been debarred from competing. Even the class for ladies' hunters had originally been restricted to male riders and it was only in 1920 that all classes were open to women.

Until the advent of Judge Wylie the standard of judging in the showjumping classes continued to be erratic and at the

Turn-out in the show ring is of paramount importance and the stables at Dublin Horse Show are a hive of activity from an early hour with exhibitors plaiting manes and tails and adding the final polish.

1919 show competitors staged an informal strike following a farcical competition on the opening day. But two years after the return of the Dublin Horse Show to the sporting calendar, Judge Wylie was appointed as chairman of the committee responsible for the reconstruction of the Ballsbridge premises. He not only successfully presented the Society's case for compensation from the military for the damages incurred during the war years, but he also set about restructuring the whole judging system in the showjumping classes. From 1921 onwards marks were awarded for each fence to a maximum of five. There was also a bonus of a further five points for spectacular rounds of jumping.

Mistakes with the forelegs were more severely penalized than faults with the hindlegs and two scorekeepers were provided to keep a tally of the results for the judges. There were still loopholes, as Judge Wylie readily admitted, but the system was established and was certainly a great deal fairer than earlier practices.

Showjumping outside Ireland was judged on an entirely different basis, with thin wooden laths on the top of every fence. If the lath was knocked, half a fault was deducted. Knockdowns with the front feet incurred four faults and with the hind two faults on a system of minus points. The proposal from a Swiss Army officer that the RDS should stage an international showjumping competition was to bring about an enormous and vital change to the sport in Ireland.

Colonel Zeigler met Judge Wylie at the Shelbourne Hotel in the autumn of 1925 and pointed out the importance of the Swiss Army as a market for the Irish horse. 'There are now on the Continent, serious rivals to this horse trade of yours, and if my country and yours could jump in friendly rivalry at Ballsbridge it would give the Irish horse the chance to show himself in world competition, and doubtless the Irish Army would participate,' the Colonel urged. Judge Wylie, however, did doubt that the Irish Army would participate. He nevertheless consulted Edward Bohane, the Director of the RDS, who thought the idea a brilliant one, and invitations for the new competition were issued.

The late Aga Khan was at that time living in Switzerland and, when Colonel Zeigler's proposal was made known to him, he immediately offered to put up a challenge trophy for the competition. So, in 1926, the first Aga Khan Cup was held at Ballsbridge (appropriately enough won by the Swiss with Ireland second of the six teams), and remains to this day one of the most prestigious contests on the Nations Cup circuit.

The introduction of the new international competition, then confined to military teams of three riders, caused a crisis within the RDS. The Society prided itself on its banks, which had to be jumped in Irish style. Horses had to change legs on the double bank, but were penalized for doing so on the single. The new competition brought the RDS into direct conflict with the rules of the sport's new governing body, the Federation Equestre Internationale (FEI) and the Society was forced to decide whether it would join the FEI or drop military jumping from its programme. The new system of Continental judging under the FEI rules made no distinction between faults with the forelegs and hindlegs, a knockdown incurring four faults, whatever the circumstances. But, more disturbing to the die-hards in the RDS, membership of the FEI would mean a departure from the Irish method of jumping banks.

After two days of argument between the warring factions, a compromise was reached whereby the natural fences of Ireland, the banks, stone wall and water, would be judged using the Irish system and the timber fences would be judged under FEI rules.

The prospect of further change was viewed with horror by

come under international rules. The removal of both the double and single banks in 1976 brought the Ballsbridge arena into line with the international system of judging, but the loss of the banks undoubtedly removed much of the character of the main showjumping arena in the RDS.

By the time the Aga Khan Cup had been added to the Horse Show programme, the RDS had undergone another internal upheaval. When Civil War broke out in June 1922 the RDS was gradually being eased out of Leinster House. Pleas that if the Society was allowed to disintegrate 'the best body that has ever been in Ireland will be utterly destroyed' met with scant sympathy and, on 14 August, the Society was informed by the Minister for Finance that the Government would be taking over the whole of Leinster House. After a considerable amount of bargaining, Judge Wylie eventually

the stalwarts of the RDS, who viewed the Dublin course as something unique. The Society continued to cling to its original rules and seemed unlikely to make any further alterations, as Terence de Vere White pointed out in his book *The Story of the Royal Dublin Society:*

In the civilian competitions the old rules persist and the Continental argument that it is too difficult to decide with which of his legs a horse has hit a fence does not carry conviction in Ireland. The rules are unlikely to be changed. Any attempt to do so at present would add the dead body of a former High Court judge to the numerous jumps that encumber the ring.

In 1948 the FEI issued new guidelines to the judges at Ballsbridge allowing them to continue 'to judge the banks of its special course according to the rules which have been in use for so long a period'. All other fences were deemed to

managed to extract £68,000 from the Government and the Society decided to concentrate all its activities at Ballsbridge from then on.

The new premises were designed by Lucius O'Callaghan, with the Horse Show grounds dominating the site. Soaring attendance figures, brought about by the introduction of the Aga Khan Cup, forced the Society to add wings to the existing grandstand and to build two completely new stands. The Irish Army Equitation School had been set up in 1926, partly in response to the challenge issued by the new team competition, but also to promote the image of the Irish horse abroad. The Army riders certainly proved that the Irish horse is a winner, notching up numerous victories during the thirties and forties following a period of intensive training from the Russian cavalry officer, Colonel Paul Rodzianko.

The Irish Army team was virtually invincible on home

OPPOSITE: Captain John Ledingham and Kilcoltrim clear the Millstreet Derby rails at the foot of the Derby bank in exemplary style. Ledingham won the 1984 Hickstead Derby and, four years later, the Millstreet Derby, both with his team horse, Gabhran.

FAR LEFT: Paul Darragh has been a regular member of the Irish team since the 1970s and was part of the quartet that claimed the Aga Khan trophy outright between 1977 and 1979.

CENTRE: Major Eddie Boylan, winner of the individual gold in the 1967 European three-day event championship on home ground at Punchestown, is still a familiar figure in the judges' box at the Dublin Horse Show.

LEFT: Eddie Macken is Ireland's best-known showjumper. He won a record four consecutive victories in the Hickstead Derby between 1976 and 1979, was twice runner-up in the world championships and also took the individual silver in the Europeans in 1977.

56

The colourful trade turnouts have only recently returned to the Dublin schedule, but have proved a popular addition to the programme.

ground, winning the Aga Khan four times in a row between 1935 and 1938, claiming the original trophy outright in 1937. Following a French victory in 1939, the competition was not held in 1940 or 1941, but the Irish squad was back in the winner's enclosure in 1942.

The names of Limerick Lace, Red Hugh, Slievenamon and Ireland's Own are on trophies from New York, Nice and Dublin, as well as the King George v Gold Cup which was won in 1935 and 1936 by the Irish Army riders, John J. Lewis claiming it in 1935 with Tramore Bay and Jed O'Dwyer riding Limerick Lace to victory the following year.

Dan Corry, who won the first running of the Dublin Grand Prix in 1930 with Slievenamon and came back to claim his second success in 1939 with Red Hugh, was still winning at international level in the fifties, bringing Ballycotton out to capture the Nice Grand Prix in 1952.

Ian Dudgeon, whose father Lieutenant Colonel Joe Hume Dudgeon was the founder of the Burton Hall riding school, also put his name on the Dublin trophy on two occasions, winning in 1950 and 1952 with Go Lightly. He was a popular competitor on the Continent as well, particularly with the Parisian crowds who went wild with delight whenever he entered the arena. Dudgeon had always assumed that this was because of the top hat which he wore in competition and was horrified to discover that the spectators proclaimed him a hero because they thought he had two artificial legs. Dudgeon did indeed have a rather awkward gait, due to injuries received during the war. But his legs were undoubtedly his own and, crooked or not, they carried him to plenty of success in the saddle. He also competed on the Irish three-day event team at the Helsinki, Stockholm and Rome Olympics.

Iris Kellett, who was to play such an important role in producing Ireland's modern-day champion Eddie Macken, became the first woman to win Dublin's feature individual class when she rode Rusty to success in 1948. It was this win that Iris Kellett still holds most dear, even though she was to go on to win the ladies' European championship twenty-one years later in the same arena at the age of forty-eight. 'No Irish competitor had even been placed at the Horse Show that year, so the crowd went absolutely wild,' she recalls. Following his win, Rusty's tail was left nearly bald after the crowds had swept into one of the outside rings where Iris and he were brought for a photo-call. Iris was rescued from the throng, but everybody wanted a hair from the tail of the Grand Prix winner.

The following year Iris and Rusty took on the top British lady riders in the first running of the Queen Elizabeth Cup, which they won. But it is the aftermath that sticks in Iris' memory, rather than the victory itself.

Iris was thoroughly briefed on the procedure for the awards ceremony. The ring stewards were determined that everything should go according to plan as the Queen herself was to present the cup to the Irish girl. Iris was instructed to dismount, leaving her horse in the capable hands of two soldiers while she went forward to Her Majesty and curtsied before the presentation. Relieved of her horse, she walked forward towards the Queen. A moment's hesitation. Do you curtsy or bow when decked out in breeches and boots? She decided on a mongrel version of the two. And it seemed to suffice as the Queen then walked forward with the beautiful new cup in her hands.

But both the stewards and the jockey failed to take into account the hypersensitive nature of the Irish horse who decided that he wanted to be part of the action as well and decided to demonstrate his resentment at being restrained in the back row by two young soldiers. Amidst great pomp and circumstance the tricolour was run up the flagpole, which was immediately behind the horses. Rusty just managed to contain himself during that. But then there was a tremendous roll of drums as the band prepared itself for playing the Irish national anthem. And that was it, Rusty could take no more. 'Being a hysterical old fool, Rusty jumped forward and pitched me straight into the Queen. I nearly knocked her over!' Profuse apologies for Rusty's behaviour to one of the stewards evoked an immediate response: 'Well what else would you expect from a Republican horse.'

Two years later Iris Kellett was back to win the cup again. But this time the awards were presented in the stand and not in the arena, obviously to prevent a repetition of the 1949 episode.

In 1953, eleven years after Iris' father Harry Kellett had helped found the strangely named Horse Jumping and Riding Encouragement Association, it was decided that the H.J. and R.E.A. should be amalgamated with the Northern Ireland Show Jumping Association to form a national organization. A meeting was arranged between the two bodies on Remembrance Day, 11 November of that year in Belfast. Representatives from the southern group had kitted themselves out with poppies especially for the occasion, but their northern counterparts, in deference to the visitors, had specifically refrained from donning their customary poppies. However, even after this inauspicious start, the meeting was a success and it was agreed that the two bodies should be amalgamated to form the Show Jumping Association of Ireland.

It was not until 1950 that the domination of the Army team was finally broken to allow civilian riders to compete in the Aga Khan Cup. However, it was to be a further thirteen years before a combined Army and civilian team managed to keep the trophy at home.

The fact that the boys from McKee Barracks got virtually every trip on offer obviously caused resentment and the story of the Army *chef d'équipe's* ducking in Rotterdam in the late

The Irish team always receives a rapturous reception from the home crowd during the parade of nations before the Aga Khan Cup at the Dublin Horse Show. Pictured here are (from left) Captain John Ledingham, Paul Darragh, Commandant Gerry Mullins and Eddie Macken.

fifties caused considerable glee amongst the civilian element. Colonel Jim Neilan had accompanied the Irish team, Army boys one and all, to a show party in Rotterdam. But his desire for a breath of fresh air during the evening got him rather more than he bargained for. As he sauntered over the beautifully manicured lawns in the garden he mistook the green surface of a watery ditch leading into one of Rotterdam's many canals for a continuation of the grass. In full dress uniform he plunged straight into the water. He eventually reappeared through the french windows covered from head to foot in slime. The rather formal party guests dissolved, *en masse*, into gales of laughter and the night took off from there. It was no consolation to the sodden Colonel that such immersions were quite frequent occurrences.

The Army riders had also completely monopolized all invitations to compete on the rich American circuit, with considerable success. Billy Ringrose, who was later to team up with the great Loch an Easpaig, won the Grand Prix in both New York and Toronto in 1956.

Diana Conolly-Carew, winner of the Dublin Grand Prix ten years later, was the only non-Army rider who managed to get away to compete in the United States, while her contemporaries Tommy Wade and Seamus Hayes, who did an inordinate amount of winning between them, missed out completely on the American invitations.

Seamus Hayes had in fact been competing in England since 1946 where, amongst his many successes with the mare Sheila, he won the leading showjumper of the year award in 1949, 1950 and 1952 at the Horse of the Year Show. Hayes returned to Ireland in the late fifties to become civilian instructor at the Army Equitation School. Two years later he started riding for wealthy Belgian owner Omer van Landeghem, who was based at Ballyboughal in north Co. Dublin. This put him back on the competitive trail where he was to join up with Leslie Fitzpatrick, Brian McNicholl and John Brooke to form the first civilian team to represent Ireland. The quartet toured the Continental circuit before competing at the world championships in Venice, won that year by Italian Raimondo d'Inzeo, who was successfully defending the title he had won four years earlier on Aachen.

Seamus Hayes, who died suddenly at the end of October 1989, will be best remembered for his partnership with the great horse Goodbye. The Hickstead Derby, which was to become virtually Irish property in the 1970s, was started in

1961 and it was Seamus and Goodbye who were to win the first running of the competition. The pair returned to take the honours three years later as well.

Eddie Macken, who was to record an incredible four successive victories over the Derby course at Hickstead during the seventies, always looked on Seamus Hayes as his hero. He still vividly remembers one occasion at Ballinamore show in Co. Longford when he was still riding 13.2 ponies. 'Seamus was riding three horses in one class and he came over and asked me to ride Goodbye around for him while he was jumping the others. I was only twelve or thirteen at the time, but it's a moment I'll never forget.'

Tommy Wade, who actually rode Goodbye for a season in 1962 before he was bought by Joe McGrath so that he could be reunited with Seamus Hayes, claims that Hayes was the best rider that Ireland has ever produced. 'He was the greatest rider of all time. I jumped against them all, the d'Inzeos, David Broome, Harvey Smith, but he was the best. He was the hardest man in the world to beat and we won't see another like him.' Oddly enough it was while Wade was riding Goodbye that he managed to beat Hayes in the Puissance at the Horse of the Year Show. Only Wade and Hayes survived to the final jump-off and both refused to divide. 'I won in the heel of the hunt,' Wade recalls.

Goodbye was second to Dundrum in Ostend when Wade had both these horses in one competition. Dundrum was also a part of Irish showjumping history and Wade still claims he was the best horse that ever came out of Ireland. Bought from between the shafts of a cart after he had bolted with the owners on board, he went on to win countless competitions on the national and international circuit. He was by the Thoroughbred sire Little Heaven out of a pure-bred Connemara mare and stood just 15.1½ hands high. Wade had his full brother as well, 'but he wasn't worth tuppence!' The little

horse was equally at home in speed classes, in Grand Prix competitions or over the Puissance wall, jumping 7ft 2in regularly. He won Grand Prix all over Europe, but was something of a Dublin specialist, winning every one of the eight classes he jumped in at the 1961 Horse Show, with Brazilian Nelson Pessoa finishing as runner-up to him in three competitions.

Wade's brushes with authority were nearly as legendary as his performances on the showgrounds of Europe. His protests that it was unfair to allow the Army riders to continue monopolizing the teams finally succeeded after he and Seamus Hayes had been forced to sit and watch the Aga Khan from the Ballsbridge competitors' stand. 'In 1963 they finally let us in and we won it.'

The four horses that had kept the trophy on home ground, Dundrum, Loch an Easpaig, Goodbye and Barrymore, reigned supreme for nearly seven years during the 1960s. Although they competed against each other throughout their careers, they only once jumped together, the combined Army and civilian quartet proving an unassailable force in the 1963 Aga Khan Cup.

Three of the great four, Dundrum, Loch an Easpaig and Goodbye, were back together again for the 1967 Aga Khan, with Ned Campion and Liathdrum making it a half-and-half Army/civilian team. The combination proved as successful as the one of four years earlier, victory this time being scored at the expense of the British.

But tragedy was to strike in the very next Nations Cup, which the Irish team contested in Ostend less than two weeks after the win in Dublin. Billy Ringrose, later to become OC of the Army Equitation School, was riding his usual partner, the wonderful Loch an Easpaig. 'He was clear in the first round,' says Ringrose. 'We walked out of the arena and, just as I stepped off, he lay down very gently, but very conclusively,

Harry Marshall endeared himself to the Dublin crowds with this piece of stunt riding at the 1989 Horse Show when Foxfield successfully cleared the Puissance wall at the winning height of 7ft 1in, only to shed his jockey before going through the finish. But if Harry's grip let him down that day, his footballing talents certainly did not.

and died.' A heart attack had cut down one of Ireland's champions in an instant.

Tommy Brennan took over as stable jockey for Omer van Landeghem when Seamus Hayes moved on. Life was pressurized there, but it brought out the best in Brennan. As well as competing at the top level of international showjumping he was to contest two Olympic Games and a world championship in three-day eventing. Only the sale of his two top showjumpers, Ambassador and Abbeville, prevented his taking on two more Olympics.

The sport of horse trials had started in Ireland with the formation of the Castletown Olympic Training and Hunter Trials Society in 1953. But in those early days, according to Brennan, 'eventing was really tied up with captains and kings. You had to have a title to compete.'

Both Brennan and his horses had a swift introduction to horse trials. After completing the one-day event at Castletown in 1963, ten years after the inaugural fixture at this lovely Co. Kildare venue, Kilbride went straight to Badminton, the premier three-day event in the world. It was at Badminton, exactly a year later, that Eddie Boylan rode Durlas Eile to victory.

Brennan took on the Badminton challenge in 1964, the year of the Tokyo Olympics, and Kilbride finished eleventh. The horse went off the boil, however, so Brennan decided that his top showjumper Kilkenny would be a better choice for the Games, even though he had never encountered a cross-country course. Kilkenny had won at Dublin that August and then had less than six weeks to acclimatize to a new sport.

Both John Harty and the brilliant Tony Cameron were clear across country. Brennan, as number three, followed team instructions for a safe clear, picking up time penalties in the process. Anchorman Harry Freeman-Jackson, winner at Burghley the previous year, could now afford to go for

individual glory. But St Finbarr uncharacteristically stopped and fell at the first fence, wrecking Ireland's chances of team or individual medals.

In spite of this disaster, the Irish team did manage to slot into fourth, with Tony Cameron riding Black Salmon into fifth in the individual. Cameron's pre-Tokyo record is worth recording. This superb all-round horseman had finished fourth in the Cheltenham Gold Cup, fourth in the Grand National and fourth at Badminton. 'We were all really on a high when we went to Tokyo,' Brennan explains. 'It was death or glory, but we missed out on the glory because we were restricted by the selectors. I just regret that I didn't ignore my instructions and let the handbrake off and really go for it.'

Kilkenny's next major outing was the World Championships at Burghley in 1966 when the Irish team of Eddie Boylan (who was to win the European title at Punchestown the following year), Ginny Freeman-Jackson, Penny Moreton and Brennan won the gold by 270 points and Ginny took the individual bronze with Sam Weller. Brennan's faithful partner was then hobdayed before being sold to American Jimmy Wofford, who rode him in two further Olympic Games, the World Championships at Punchestown in 1970 and three Pan American Games, proving the stamina and longevity of the Irish-bred horse.

In 1968 Brennan, who had by then left Omer van Landeghem's Skidoo Stud, was selected for the Olympic Games in Mexico. But he was not picked for the three-day eventing squad. He would be travelling with Tubbermac as a member of the showjumping team. In the build-up to the Games Brennan and Tubbermac were part of that year's Aga Khan Cup team, bidding to retain the trophy after the 1967 victory. Tragically, Tubbermac skidded and fell on the sharp turn after the water jump, breaking his back and leg in the process, and had to be shot.

Minus his horse Brennan was still selected as reserve rider for the showjumpers. He wound up in the eventing squad, however, after a series of mishaps which left him riding March Hawk, a horse that had managed to break a leg apiece for two previous jockeys and the arm of a third. Not terribly keen on the prospect, Brennan nevertheless sat up on horse for the first time two days before the start of the competition. Rain — unbelievable downpours that started precisely at four in the afternoon and ended equally abruptly at six — were the feature of the Mexico Olympics. But there seemed to be no question of the organizers altering the timetable to try and miss the worst of the weather.

The showjumping team of Diana Conolly-Carew, Ada Matheson and Ned Campion were eliminated and the three-day eventers were to suffer a similar fate, although in far more dramatic circumstances. The Irish team was lying third after the dressage, but all hopes of a medal were to disappear on cross-country day. Penny Moreton's Loughlin, a member of the squad that had won the World Championships at Burghley two years earlier, was renowned for his brilliance over the solid timber. But his exuberance was to be his downfall and, overjumping on the cross-country, he fell and was killed instantly.

Juliet Jobling-Purser also became victim to an excess of jumping ability when her mare Jenny jumped her straight out of the saddle. The mare disappeared out into the country and it was some time before she was retrieved to be reunited with her jockey. Diana Wilson and Chianti Rosso boosted the flagging Irish morale with a clear. But then the rain started.

Brennan was third last to go with March Hawk. 'I knew as I was starting that I had no chance of survival,' he says. He got as far as the seventh fence, a rail in water. But, in appalling floods, March Hawk never even saw the fence and fell into the swirling torrents. Brennan, unable to swim, was caught by the current and seemed about to be swept away when the fates stepped in, obviously weary of kicking the Irish in the teeth. Instead of vanishing downstream, Brennan was carried straight into his horse who was valiantly struggling out at the far side. Somehow Tommy managed to clamber aboard and heroically continued on the course, but only as far as the next fence. March Hawk, with his lungs half full of water, fell straight into the open ditch. He was rescued by Prince Philip, who happened to be there as a spectator and pulled the horse out. At this stage Brennan decided enough was enough. Neither of the remaining two horses managed to complete.

Five riders were taken to hospital by helicopter, two horses were killed during the day, and March Hawk was to die on his return to Ireland. The eventual winners, Sergeant Ben Jones and Barbary, deserved a double gold medal, according to Tommy Brennan. 'They went just before me and swam their way round. It was in fact an easy course on perfect going, until the rain.'

Mexico signalled the end of Brennan's eventing career. The Irish team recovered to win two European team bronzes in the intervening years before John Watson collected the world individual silver at Lexington in 1978. Twelve months later Watson was on the squad that took the European gold in Luhmuhlen, but this was followed by a very lean period which only came to an end in 1989 when Joe McGowan, fifth individually, led the team to the European bronze at Burghley. On home ground at Punchestown in 1991 the Irish took the team silver to add to Ireland's first ever junior individual gold, won by sixteen-year-old Suzanne Donnelly to help the Irish to the team bronze at the junior championships in Rotherfield Park two weeks earlier.

Tommy Brennan may have finished with the eventing world, but he still had plenty of showjumping wins in him, teaming up with Frank Kernan from Crossmaglen, one of Ireland's best known dealers. Kernan gave Brennan the ride on such horses as Ambassador, Marcella — the brilliant mare who won so many hot classes — Top of the Morning and Prosperous. Ambassador was an obvious candidate for the showjumping at the 1972 Games in Munich and Kernan was keen to keep the horse for Brennan to ride. But although Ambassador and Brennan claimed fourteen major Grand Prix classes in one season, Kernan was unable to get sponsorship to retain the horse in Ireland. When a very attractive offer was made for the horse by Italian ace Graziano Mancinelli, Kernan felt unable to turn it down. Ambassador and his new jockey went on to win the individual gold in Munich.

Showing may be a serious business at Dublin which involves months of preparation, but there is always time for a joke before the measuring stick is used as the final arbiter.

Dublin always attracts a good international field for the showjumping and there is usually a line-out of five teams for the Nations Cup on the Friday of Horse Show week when the Aga Khan trophy is at stake.

Brennan then left his base in Malahide and moved his horses to Abbeville, home of the future Fianna Fail leader and Irish Prime Minister, Charles Haughey. It was here that he took on another outstanding mare, Abbeville. Still only Grade B, the mare travelled to Wiesbaden in 1974 where she was instantly snapped up by Germany's Alwin Schockemohle. Brennan and the mare were booked to ride on the Nations Cup team at Lucerne, so Abbeville remained in the Irish camp for another week before being sent to her new home in Germany. Brennan retired from showjumping immediately after Lucerne.

Despite Brennan's retirement the mare continued to promote Irish breeding for another fifteen years. Although the new partnership with Schockemohle failed to gel, Abbeville enjoyed unprecedented success with Brazilian rider Nelson Pessoa. Her name was changed to Miss Moet, following sponsorship from Moet et Chandon, and although name changes are supposed to be unlucky, the former Abbeville went on to win an unbelievable 173 Puissance classes. She was undoubtedly the best Puissance horse ever foaled. Following her retirement, Abbeville was officially returned to her breeder at the 1989 Kerrygold Dublin Horse Show, in foal to the Thoroughbred stallion Andretti, which stands at Ballinabanogue Stud in Co. Waterford, the home of Abbeville's own sire Nordlys.

Abbeville had nearly been sold to the Army Equitation School, but when this deal fell through, her owner Charles Haughey decided to try and keep her for the 1976 Olympics in Montreal. However, shortly before Brennan and the mare headed off for Lucerne in 1974, the Irish Federation decided to implement a ruling imposed by the FEI that only riders with amateur licences could ride at the Games. Brennan had been furnished with the required amateur licence by the Irish Federation but, a week before he was due to leave for the Continental show circuit, it was rescinded and replaced with a professional licence because he was trading in horses in his capacity as a director of Dublin Bloodstock. The case was referred to the High Court, which found in favour of Brennan. Shortly after this victory, however, the FEI stated that riders trading in horses were to be deemed professional.

Brennan still smarts under the injustice of a system that saw all the top Irish and British riders declared professional, while

ABOVE: *The dressage discipline in the three-day event may not be of Grand Prix standard, but it is equally difficult to perform a good test with a horse tuned to gallop over a 4½-mile cross-country course of around thirty solid fences like the one at Punchestown, venue for the 1991 European championships.*

OPPOSITE: *The Heineken water at the Punchestown international three-day event is always the focal point on the cross-country course, both for the competitors and the spectators. Exciting action is guaranteed and the crowds get real value for their money without even moving, as the course doubles back to the water for the second-last fence.*

the Continentals continued to disregard the new ruling. 'All the opposition were top professionals and, while we were sitting at home they were going out and winning the medals. Gerd Wiltfang, who had been on the German team that won the gold in Munich, was described as a car-park attendant! The Irish and British were crucified by their Federations, so I decided the time had come to give up.'

Eddie Macken, the world's most stylish horseman, was to be dealt the same blow when he, too, was declared professional by the Irish Federation. Although he kicked against the traces because of the ban on riding foreign-bred horses (the resulting case was eventually settled in Macken's favour on the steps of the European Court), he never resented the fact that he was debarred from the Olympic Games. 'The world championships were the major event then. I knew there was never any chance of going to the Olympics so it was never really a disappointment. But it was a hasty decision by the Irish and English Federations and, unfortunately, the other countries didn't follow suit. In hindsight it should never have happened.'

When the ban on professional riders was lifted for the 1988 Olympics in Seoul, it was too late for Macken. His top horse, the classic showjumper Boomerang, had retired in 1980 and Macken has found nothing of his calibre since. 'I would love to go to the Games, but only if I thought I was in with a chance. I certainly wouldn't go just for the sake of competing in an Olympics.'

The days of the brilliant Boomerang are hard ones to recreate. Having been rejected as a second string speed horse, Boomerang was given to Macken by Paul Schockemohle to use 'until he found something better'. Macken in fact had originally ridden the horse as a youngster during his six-year stint with Iris Kellett in Mespil Hall in Dublin. Boomerang was then sold, through Tommy Brennan, to Ted Edgar whose wife Liz won a lot of speed classes with him, as did his next rider, Dutchman Johan Heins.

Macken had moved to Germany to work with Paul Schockemohle in the spring of 1975 and it was later that year that he was given the ride on Boomerang. Their first show together was Wiesbaden where the 24-year-old Macken qualified for the Grand Prix. It was the Grand Prix debut of both horse and rider but, not only did they survive the ordeal, they won to set the stage for the next five years when the pair would dominate Grand Prix competition throughout the world.

Until his departure for Germany, Macken's international experience had been limited to Hickstead, Ostend, Rotterdam and of course Dublin, where he first rode on the Aga Khan Cup team in 1970. He had gone to Iris Kellett a year earlier for a six-month course which would hopefully allow him to produce a few horses to bolster up the income on the family farm in Granard, Co. Longford. 'I went for six months and ended up staying six years.' Those six years under the critical eye of one of the world's greatest trainers were to stand Macken in good stead as he embarked on his international career. Riding Pele, Oatfield Hills and Easter Parade for Iris, Macken was winning virtually everything in Ireland.

He put in a good showing at the 1973 European championships in Hickstead, finishing ninth with Oatfield Hills behind Paddy McMahon and the Irish-bred Pennwood Forge Mill. The following year he returned to the Sussex showground with Pele for the world championships. Macken was horrified by the size of the courses, but he and Pele put up a tremendous battle, forcing Hartwig Steenken and Simona to a jump-off for the title. Macken was drawn first to go and, with two fences down, as good as handed the championships to the German. Steenken also failed to go clear, but with only a single error, he claimed the gold medal leaving the young pretender with the silver. 'I was never really disappointed at not winning in 1974. I was pleased to have done as well as I did. It was a sort of dream, but I didn't deserve to win.

A first prize in the showing classes at Dublin is a much sought-after commodity, particularly in the youngstock division, where the judges have the unenviable task of trying to pick a winner from as many as forty well-bred and beautifully produced youngsters.

Drink, religion and horses have featured in the lives of the Irish people for centuries.

Hartwig and Simona were the outstanding combination and they did deserve to take the title.'

He was also to be the European silver medallist at Vienna in 1977 in the build-up to the world challenge the following year. Riding Pele (who had now been renamed Kerrygold following sponsorship from Bord Bainne, the Irish Dairy Board), Macken jumped his way up the order over the three days of the championship to wind up sharing the lead with Dutch rider Johan Heins. The luck of the draw was against Macken yet again when he had to go first in the jump-off. His target of four faults in 51.5 seconds left Heins with the agonizing choice of going for a careful clear or aiming to beat Macken's time. He went for the time, hit a fence in the process, but still managed to snatch the gold and its accompanying title by a mere tenth of a second.

Boomerang had been considered too short of scope to tackle the courses at Vienna. But a year later, flying a new banner for the cigarette company, P. J. Carroll and Co., which had also taken on Paul Darragh's string, Boomerang was Macken's choice for his next crack at the world championships in Aachen in 1978. The horse had by now more than proved his ability, winning three consecutive Hickstead Derbys (he was to add a record fourth 12 months later) and a Hamburg Derby, as well as numerous Grand Prix. For good measure he had already proved that Aachen was a lucky showground for him by claiming both the Grand Prix and the championship, an unprecedented double, at the Nations Cup show held earlier in 1978.

Macken was fourth after the first leg of the championships, a speed class, moved up to third on the second day to qualify for the final in which the top four all ride each other's horses, only to be beaten a short head at the finish yet again. 'The sequence was right,' said Macken afterwards, 'but the post came too soon.' Macken was first to ride the Dutch-bred Pandur Z, the horse belonging to his old rival Johan Heins. 'He was a big, strong horse, but very deceptive. He was incredibly sensitive and just froze when I got on him. I spent the first part of the course just trying to get him into a nice rhythm and settle him. I got that, but it meant I was just a bit too slow.' Agonizingly close to the time allowed, Macken picked up the smallest fraction possible in showjumping, a quarter of a time fault, to mar an otherwise perfect round. Clear with his own horse and the remaining two finalists, he could only sit and watch while another German snatched yet another world title from his grasp.

Gerd Wiltfang conjured up four faultless rounds to win the gold. Both Wiltfang's horse Roman and Boomerang were clear throughout the finals, a feat rarely accomplished in the often criticised format of the world championships. (The magnificent Rockbarton, who did so much winning for his two Army riders Con Power and Gerry Mullins, came close

to mirroring this performance in the 1982 championships in Dublin, faulting only with Mullins, his everyday partner to finish just out of the medals in fourth.) 'That was definitely my biggest disappointment. Boomerang had done everything to win it. He was the best horse in Europe at the time. Me having a time fault on the other horse denied him the chance of being world champion. It's still my greatest regret. He did everything bar win it, but it just wasn't to be.'

It was not to be the following year either when a controversial foot in the water kept him down in fourth place in the European championships at Rotterdam in what would otherwise have been a winning performance.

However, the Battleburn gelding did more than his share of winning outside the elusive sphere of the championships. The sheer consistency of Boomerang's performances made him into the biggest money-spinner of the seventies when he totted up over £250,000 in prize-money, a record at that

OPPOSITE: *The Army Equitation School, in the heart of Dublin, provided Ireland's first showjumping team for the inaugural Aga Khan Cup at the Dublin Horse Show in 1926, which was open only to military teams of three riders.*

BELOW: *As well as the international showjumping arena, the Royal Dublin Society showgrounds at Ballsbridge boast three other showing rings, a warm-up arena, a veterinary paddock and, in the Simmonscourt extension, the national jumping arena.*

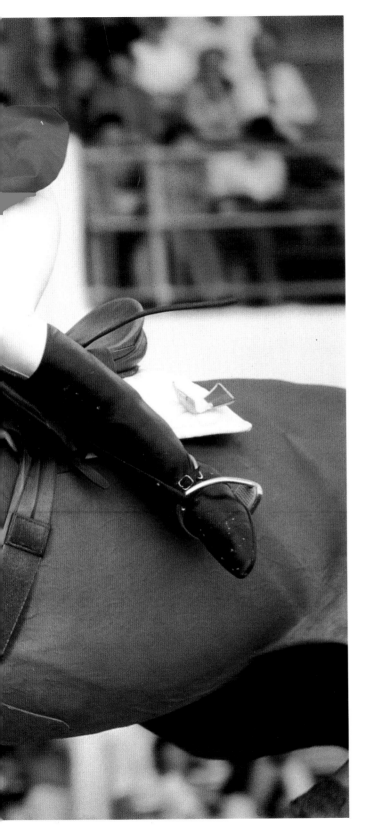

time, although virtually eclipsed by the incredible Milton who will undoubtedly break the £1 million barrier. Boomerang's four consecutive Hickstead Derby victories between 1976 and 1979 have never been equalled, let alone surpassed and, on two of those occasions, in 1976 and 1978, his name was added to the elite band of horses that have jumped clear round this challenging track.

Retired in 1980, Boomerang finally had to be put down on 20 May 1983. He is buried at Macken's Rafeehan Stud just outside Kells. Described as the Milton of the 1970s by his rider, Boomerang is commemorated by the beautiful trophy that is now presented to the winner of the Hickstead Derby, a bronze which depicts Macken and the great horse coming down the Derby Bank – a fitting tribute to one of the all-time greats of Irish showjumping. (This very special trophy took pride of place in the officers' mess at McKee Barracks, home of the Army Equitation School, when Captain John Ledingham won at Hickstead with Gabhran in 1984.)

But where are the replacements for such horses? Have they all been sold abroad to win glory for other nations? 'When we won the Aga Khan outright in 1979 it was pure chance that the likes of Boomerang, Heather Honey, Rockbarton and Condy came together,' says Macken. 'Everybody sat back and basked in the reflected glory. It was the same with Goodbye, Dundrum, Loch an Easpaig and Barrymore. What we need now is some form of Government subsidy to keep the good horses in Ireland for our talented young riders. We breed horses to sell them. But there isn't enough importance put on the shop window. Horses and Ireland are so closely associated and an Irish team competing and winning on the Continent has to be the best ambassador there is, both for Ireland and the Irish horse.'

CHAPTER FOUR

FLAT RACING

*F*LAT RACING in Ireland is in a constant state of flux. During the late 1980s the glamorous face of the sport, the race meetings themselves, presented a healthy image. The injection of huge capital from the Middle East was bolstering up a business that had been through some lean times in the seventies with the oil crisis and the mid-eighties when bloodstock prices were hit by a major recession which saw the top Irish vendors selling in England rather than on the home market.

But behind the scenes, the rot has begun to eat away at the very fabric of the industry. In the previous half century the country has lost nine race tracks and, of the twenty-seven remaining, the majority are in a sad state of repair. Most of them have been in existence since the turn of the century or before, and expensive refits have been carried out on only a small percentage with the result that the worst ravages of time are beginning to show all too plainly.

The Killanin report of 1986 estimated that complete modernization of the country's racecourses would cost in the region of £25 million. It also recommended that racecourse improvements should take priority over increased prize-money. At the time of the report three race tracks, the Curragh, Leopardstown and Phoenix Park, absorbed 58 per cent of the prize-money on offer in Ireland. All three have received extensive refurbishment yet, despite the money poured into its facelift, the Phoenix Park could survive no longer than the first ten months of the nineties.

The unfair division of wealth is all too obvious. Yet the sport continues to attract the punters, even to the less fashionable tracks where the prize-money fails to lure the glitterati of the game. The entertainment on offer is vastly differing but, of those twenty-seven tracks, all bar two hold meetings under both Rules. The exceptions are Kilbeggan, in the very heart of Ireland, which holds only National Hunt meetings, and Laytown which, for the simple reason that its one meeting of the year is held on a beach, is exclusively flat.

Racing on the flat is undoubtedly the more glamorous side of the sport, but there is also no doubt that the Irish revel in the jump meetings and have produced a breed of horse that excels itself over fences. Even so, any race meeting in Ireland will draw crowds, whether there are fences to be jumped or not, and mixed meetings are tailor-made to suit all tastes.

---

*OPPOSITE: **The starting stalls.** ABOVE: Racegoers at the Nun Run at Trim in Co. Meath.*

Not everyone is totally engrossed in the horse flesh, so there must be something to be said for aerial advertising after all.

As a nation the Irish love to dress up. And where better to parade the finery than at the Curragh, home of the Irish Derby? The glamour on display may not quite put Royal Ascot to shame, but it does its best to rival it, even though the only royals likely to grace the scene are a sprinkling of sheikhs.

The predecessor of the Irish Derby dates back as far as 1817 when, inspired by the undoubted success of the Epsom race, the Irish Turf Club instituted the O'Darby Stakes. The new race was run in June of that year, at the Curragh, and was won by Souvenir. But it failed to capture the imagination of the public and, seven years later, it was abandoned. The Turf Club were not keen to let the idea drop however and, in 1848, made a second attempt, this time with the Curragh Derby. With bitter-sweet irony this new addition to the calendar was won by a horse called Justice to Ireland. But both the race and the ideal behind the winner's name were to prove short-lived and the Derby once again vanished from the Irish racing scene.

Whether it was third time lucky or not, the next attempt to introduce the Derby to Ireland finally succeeded with the start of the Irish Derby Sweepstakes in June 1866. The Derby

In the first ten years of the new race the biggest field was just six runners, that number coming under starter's orders in 1869, the year in which the Turf Club added an extra 100 sovereigns to the stakes. This, however, was a considerable improvement on the previous year when only two had gone to post. It seemed that the popular favourite Bee Quick would gallop his sole rival Madeira into the ground and his price of 3/1 on seemed more than generous. But Bee Quick failed to live up to either his name or his reputation and Madeira went on to win at a canter by more than 6 lengths.

Things seemed to have improved by 1879, however, when eight horses paraded for the fourteenth running of the Irish Derby. But although all eight started, it was a two-horse race from the outset, with the joint-favourite Soulouque coming home a length to the good from Shinglass, who had shared the winner's starting price of 100/30.

The following year an unprecedented prize fund of 550 sovereigns drew a field of eleven runners and a huge crowd. The Irish Derby, fourteen years after the Turf Club added it to the calendar for the third time, had finally become an established fixture and had joined the big National Hunt festival at Punchestown as one of the major social occasions of the year.

Flat racing preceded its more hazardous counterpart by more than a century. One of the first officially recorded races

meeting at the Curragh had been advertized in 1864 and, although shunned by owners and trainers, unanimously decried by the press and invariably producing little or no sport, it became an almost instant social success, a feature which it has retained up to modern times.

In those early days, in the second half of the nineteenth century, the Derby still seemed doomed. The addition of extra prize-money in 1869 still failed to attract a decent field, as did the amended distance three years later and the altered conditions in 1874 which, in the form of a handicap, extended the weight range to an incredible 36lb.

Lay in sterling, pay in sterling, or stick to Irish pounds to do your winning – the bookies do not mind as long as you put your money on something.

was contested at the Curragh in 1640 for a Plate of forty sovereigns donated by the Trustees of the Duke of Leinster. But if this was an organized race, then disorganized racing had been going on since almost the dawn of civilization. Irish warriors of the third century AD pitted their chargers against each other, while the ordinary country folk held horse races at fairs. Probably the best known fair was held at the Curragh, thought to be derived from the Gaelic *currech*, which means a racecourse, rather than the other Gaelic word *curragh*, meaning a marsh. But beaches, or strands as they are known in Ireland, were also popular venues for races.

Saddles were unknown in the earliest records of horse racing and even bridles were mere halters, with a stout stick being used to guide the horse. However, the fourteenth-century Statute of Kilkenny expressly forbad Englishmen, with land or rent to the value of £100 per year, from riding in the Irish style. Any Englishman found riding without a saddle was required to forfeit his horse to the King and his body to prison, until a fine deemed suitable by His Majesty had been paid. This law was repealed in 1495, but was brought back into force by Henry VIII less than thirty years later.

The Irish hobby, which is thought to have come originally from Spain, was used for racing, even though it stood only around 13 hands high. These hobbies were considered extremely valuable, and were exported in great numbers to England. But their qualities were obviously mixed, as they were described, 'in racing wonderful swift, in gallop false and indifferent'.

Racing was held mainly on Sundays and, although Cromwell and the ways of Puritanism combined forces to try and prevent these goings-on, the sport managed to survive. Sunday racing has now returned to the calendar, reappearing in Ireland in 1985 after protracted negotiations with the unions, most of which were not motivated by religious ideals.

Bellewstown, in Co. Meath, held its first race meetings during the 1630s and still flourishes today, with its three-day fixture in July attracting great crowds. The meeting combines flat races and hurdles, as the jumping season spans the entire year in Ireland.

Racing in the north of Ireland was also well established by the middle of the seventeenth century. Meetings had been held at the Maze from 1640 onwards. But religion imposed its own regulations here as well when, shortly after the Jockey Club was founded in England more than a century later, the new body allowed the northern stewards to insist that all starters should carry a Bible. This was a contingency against problems arising from a false start, in which case the starter would be required to swear on the Bible that he had not given the signal to start.

During the 1670s three days of racing, followed by a horse fair, were established by Sir William Temple, then Provost of Trinity College. Two King's Plates were to be awarded in each race, the winner receiving £30 and the second £20. King Charles II duly provided the two plates, which were competed for annually, in April and September, at the Curragh. The Earl of Clarendon was reported to have been appalled by the unruliness of the race meetings, but was obviously impressed with the Curragh, which he described as 'much finer turf than Newmarket'.

The outbreak of war, brought about by the 1688 Revolution and the resulting Battle of the Boyne, effectively prevented any further development in the racing world. The Penal Laws, under which it was an offence for any Catholic to own or keep a horse worth £5 or more, also hindered progress. But there were always ways round these laws, even though they stated that any Protestant could report transgressors to two Justices of the Peace and then claim the horse for himself, on the payment of £5. Another law that was blatantly flouted was one that was passed in 1739, prohibiting matches between horses and making it illegal to run for plates worth less than £120.

But towards the middle of the eighteenth century, racing was spreading throughout Ireland and, when John Cheney produced his racing calendar of 1741 (first published in 1727), he recorded advertisements for racing at Mullingar, Mallow and Limerick. However, these meetings all had to be postponed to the following year due to a lack of starters.

In 1745 a grey mare called Irish Lass won the Royal Plate at the Curragh. When she won the same race again two years later for her owner Mr Archbold of Eadestown, Co. Kildare,

BELOW: Sheikh Maktoum and trainer Henry Cecil (far right) are interviewed by the international press after Old Vic's win in the 1989 Budweiser Irish Derby.

Sir Ralph Gore challenged Mr Archbold to a match against his own horse Black and All Black. Sir Ralph's horse had been exported from England where it had raced successfully under the name of Othello. But his challenge failed to pay dividends, in spite of the fact that Black and All Black started as favourite.

The mare went on to win and many of the superstitious bystanders attributed her success to the string of rosary beads that had been put round her neck at the start. The Irish for rosary is *paidrin*, and Irish Lass immediately became known as the Paidrin mare, entering the realms of Irish folklore. Oliver Goldsmith was to write about her in 1757, complaining peevishly, 'there has been more money spent in the encouragement of the Paidrin mare there in one season than in rewards given to learned men since the times of Ussher.' The mare's victory also seemed to confirm the opinion of James I that all Irish horses were Papists, as he had been heard to swear when presented with an Irish horse by Deputy Lord Chichester.

But, according to folklore, the Paidrin mare did not benefit by her win. When she appeared at the next race meeting, her owner was arrested by the stewards and the mare was shot on the course. The mare was cut open and, it was said, a pair of

wings was found attached to her heart. It was these wings that were believed to have helped her win the race against Black and All Black, the embodiment of evil.

But the mare's vanquished rival continued his racing career, being matched in 1751 against the Earl of March's Bajazet. The stakes were 1,000 guineas with a further 10,000 guineas in side bets. Black and All Black thoroughly redeemed himself by winning this match, in spite of the best efforts of Lord March, whose jockey was instructed to weigh out with a belt filled with lead shot. This was ditched at the start and was handed back by an accomplice before the jockey weighed in after the race. But Sir Ralph was too clever to be caught out in this fashion and, even though his own horse had won, he managed to extract a confession from the terrified jockey, who had no qualms about implicating his employer. A challenge for a duel was then issued for five o'clock the following morning.

Lord March's apparently renowned cowardice under fire received another nasty jolt when he appeared at the chosen spot. Sir Ralph duly arrived, bearing with him a polished oak coffin, which was placed, with the lid open, facing towards Lord March. The inscription on the lid gave Lord March's name, date of birth and the date of his death – the very day of the duel. When Sir Ralph then casually informed his opponent that he never missed his man, Lord March instantly confessed to the crime and offered his apologies.

The Jockey Club had been set up in England the year before Black and All Black met Bajazet on the 4-mile course at the Curragh. Six years later, Lord March was elected as one of the new body's earliest members and, almost immediately, he set about introducing new rulings which would ensure that jockeys carried the correct weight!

Although Cheney's calendar of 1741 had listed only eleven meetings in Ireland, by the time the English Jockey Club had been founded in 1750 there were seventy-one Irish fixtures advertised and there were obviously plenty more that had not attracted the attention of Cheney. It was to be another forty years, however, before a similar body to the Jockey Club was set up in Ireland. The first volume of the Irish Racing Calendar, dated 1790 and edited by Pat Sharkey, incorporated the Rules and Orders of the Irish Turf Club. The new body governed the rules of racing on the Curragh and eventually formed the basis of rules for racing throughout Ireland.

The introduction of Turf Club stewards, three for each meeting, was one of the first moves made by the new body. The stewards were responsible for settling all disputes and, in the event of the modern-day equivalent of a photo-finish (although obviously without the benefit of a camera), the stewards could make the dead-heaters run again for the prize, after the last race of the day.

The valets are responsible for all the jockeys' gear, including breeches, boots, silks and saddles, as well as lead cloths on the National Hunt circuit. Valet's assistant Sean Duffy gets the occasional break for a cup of tea and a chat, although his companion here, Paul Coyle, was forced into retirement by a back injury in 1990.

The champagne bar at the Curragh on Derby day always does a roaring trade.

Racing had certainly undergone some dramatic changes since the ruling in 1734 which stated, 'no jostling to be allow'd except in the last half mile of each heat.' These heats were usually run over a mile, but horses would frequently run in as many as four during the course of a day.

The Irish Racing Calendar named eighteen racecourses which came under the jurisdiction of the Turf Club. Each track was allocated one meeting a year, with the exception of the Curragh which was allowed two meetings in April and one in June, September and October. The Calendar for 1790 also listed twenty-two race meetings for the year. Week-long fixtures were fairly common at this time, but the Curragh's final meeting of the season was more like a marathon, lasting from 25 October to 5 November, twelve days of racing.

The Curragh had long been the established headquarters of racing in Ireland and, in the second half of the eighteenth century, it became common practice for members of the ascendancy to build lodges on the edge of Curragh. The Lords had their horses trained on these premises and would use the accommodation themselves for race meetings. It was not until the turn of the century that the first public trainer appeared on the scene. This was Pat Connolly, who had started life as a training groom, but who then took over Waterford Lodge in 1812 as Ireland's first independent trainer.

The O'Darby Stakes, which had been instituted to bolster up the Curragh's June meeting, was in its final death throes when King George IV paid a visit to the course in September 1821. At the time the King was suffering from a tiresome bout of 'wherry-go-nimbles', which Colonel S. J. Watson, in his excellent work on the history of Irish steeplechasing *Between the Flags* attributed to 'over-lavish fare at the banquets, or under-lavish hygiene in the kitchen'. The Duke of Leinster was dispatched post-haste to Dublin to procure a water closet for the royal personage from a Mr Simmons, the acknowledged expert in these areas. All was duly accomplished and the King was received with great pomp and circumstance into the specially erected stand and banqueting room. Presumably all was found to be satisfactory, as the King presented a gold whip to the Duke of Leinster just before he left the racecourse. The King also offered stakes of £100 a year which, along with the golden whip, were to be raced for annually at the Curragh on a handicap basis.

In 1833 a horse that was to have an enormous influence on the Irish bloodstock industry was foaled at Brownstown House on the Curragh. This was Birdcatcher, who was sold as a yearling to neighbouring trainer William Disney. Birdcatcher won three races as a three-year-old, including the Peel challenge cup in which he stormed past the post, more than 500 yards to the good, and then proceeded to bolt on into Newbridge, nearly 2 miles away.

But it was his performance at stud that marked Birdcatcher out as one of the most influential horses of the age. He sired the Derby winner Daniel O'Rourke, two St Leger winners, Knight of St George and The Baron, as well as two winners of the Oaks. Classic winners throughout the middle years of the nineteenth century could be traced back to Birdcatcher who, along with Harkaway, one of the most prolific winners of this era, did more to advertise the Irish Thoroughbred than virtually any other horse in the country.

The advancement of the railway now made racing more accessible and, when the Turf Club ran the first Irish Derby Sweepstakes at the Curragh in June 1866, a race special of thirty carriages was put on to transport the Dublin punters from Kingsbridge station to the Curragh. The result was record crowds at the meeting. Unfortunately the runners for the new race failed to follow suit. Only three came under starter's orders for the Derby, which was won by the English-owned but Dublin-bred Selim, ridden by 'Lucky' Charlie Maidment, who was to be champion jockey in Ireland in both 1866 and 1867.

James Cockin's Selim, who like all Cockin's horses was used to an arduous schedule, had had an easy day of it on the eve of the feature race when he had been awarded a walk-over as his rivals had failed to get to the post in time. He started as second favourite for the Derby, just behind the then unnamed Tom King in the market. Making all the running, Selim won, going away by more than 3 lengths. The following day Selim and Tom King met again, in a 3-mile Queen's Plate and, once again, Selim came home first. On the final day of the meeting Selim was back in the winner's enclosure after holding off all challengers in a 4-mile plate.

But this was not Cockin's first raid on Irish soil. He had campaigned Lord Conyngham the previous season to corner seven Queen's Plates. The stewards of the Turf Club promptly altered the rules to prohibit horses that had been brought over from England with a specific race as their goal. From now on only horses that had been in training in Ireland six months prior to the race could be declared. This ruling came into effect in 1868, by which time Cockin had also taken the second running of the Irish Derby with Golden Plover, the 7/4 favourite who won at a canter, as well as two other races that day. Despite the best efforts of the authorities, Cockin was leading owner in Ireland seven times during the 1860s.

Cockin was by no means put out by the Turf Club's attempts to oust him from the winners' enclosures of Ireland. He simply bought the mare Aneroid from Curragh trainer Pat Doucie and carried on his winning ways. The mare went on to serve her owner well at stud, producing Inishowen who won the 1875 Derby for Cockin, the English raider's third victory in the Curragh's feature race. Inishowen was by Uncas,

another of Cockin's successful string, although he too suffered from being raced too often and too early. But the horse flourished once retired to stud and was to sire four winners of the Irish Derby.

The Curragh was unquestionably the centre of Irish racing and was now rivalling Punchestown as the main social occasion of the year. By the middle of the nineteenth century there were no less than twenty-five courses used regularly on the Curragh, ranging from a 2 furlong 147 yard track for yearlings to a full 4-mile course.

Other 'enclosed' courses were now beginning to appear. The inaugural meeting at Baldoyle was held in March 1860 and, as one of the earliest of the new courses, Baldoyle managed to earmark all the best dates on the calendar. The

first fixture was publicized as the Howth and Baldoyle Race Meeting, but by 1868 the reference to Howth had been dropped. Twelve years later the name was changed again to the Dublin Metropolitan Races and the first Baldoyle Derby was run at the May meeting. This was introduced as a direct rival to the Curragh Derby. Run over 3 miles, with colts to carry 8st 10lb and fillies 8st 7lb, it was viewed by many trainers as a truer test than the Curragh race. As a result the Baldoyle Derby eclipsed the Curragh equivalent for several years.

Racing in the west of Ireland had long been established. A five-day meeting at Knockbarron, near Loughrea, is recorded in 1764. But it was in August 1869 that the present racecourse at Ballybrit, near Galway, was first opened to an obviously

ABOVE AND FOLLOWING PAGE: The mountains of Mourne do sweep down to the sea, but not actually at Laytown where racing is held on the beach itself and the starting time of the meeting is dictated by the tide. The first officially recorded meeting on the strand at Laytown was in 1876.

apreciative public, as 40,000 people turned out for the occasion.

Racing was held in Mayo during the 1830s and, in 1834, meetings were staged at both Ballinrobe and Tuam, although the chief attraction at most of these western fixtures was steeplechasing rather than flat racing.

Wagers had been made amongst the monied classes for many years. But the less wealthy got their chance to bet with the arrival of one of the first bookmakers in Ireland, Paddy Keary, owner of the 1870 Irish Derby winner Billy Pitt. He was nicknamed Bank of Ireland Keary because he settled his debts exclusively in Bank of Ireland notes.

The 1871 Derby winner was Maid of Athens, a mare by

The stewards' vantage point at the Curragh, home of all the Irish Classics.

Solon, who was also to sire Barcaldine, a horse that was to take over the mantle of Birdcatcher and Harkaway, and who was claimed to be the finest racehorse to come out of Ireland in the latter part of the nineteenth century. Solon himself was an outstanding stallion, also siring Sylph, winner of the 1883 Irish Derby, as well as numerous other top-class progeny. Solon was out of a mare by Birdcatcher.

But it was his son Barcaldine who was to capture the attention of the racing public. Unbeaten as a two-year-old, Barcaldine came out in the spring of 1881 to slaughter the opposition in the Baldoyle Derby. Hearing rumours that he was about to be warned off for scratching his horse in return for financial reward, Barcaldine's owner George Low decided to try and recoup some of his losses before they occurred. He ran Barcaldine on three successive days at the Curragh June meeting, winning on the first two and then being given a walk-over on the third when the other declared runners declined to take him on. As predicted, Low was warned off by the authorities and, after various attempts to run Barcaldine under patently false ownership, the horse was finally sold to English trainer Robert Peck, for whom he won four races before breaking down and being retired to stud.

As a stallion Barcaldine was to sire Sir Visto, winner of the Derby and St Leger; Mist, winner of the 1,000 Guineas and the Oaks; and Marco, himself a big winner, but also the sire of Marcovil. In his turn, Marcovil was to produce Hurry On and My Prince, two of the most prepotent stallions of the new century.

Although some of the older racecourses, such as Cashel and Newcastle, had vanished, by the mid-1870s Tramore, Cork Park and Galway were all in existence and the Wexford track was built on reclaimed sloblands.

Racing was a national pastime which brought together all levels of society. Even the man who was to become the champion of Home Rule in the following decade, Charles Stewart Parnell, was involved and is named as one of the stewards at Laytown in September 1876. This was the first recorded meeting on the strand at Laytown. This race meeting was started by the local parish priest as a way of augmenting church funds, until his puritanically minded bishop put a stop to such frivolity. Racing at Laytown was held only irregularly until the early twentieth century when the Delaney family took it over. The original enclosure at Laytown was actually Paddy Delaney's lawn, but a 3-acre field adjoining the dunes now houses the parade ring and the bookmakers' stands.

In August 1888 Dublin's Leopardstown racecourse was opened, but it was declared an unmitigated disaster by press and public alike when enthusiasm to see the new track totally swamped all methods of transport and the facilities at the course itself. In spite of this inauspicious debut, Leopardstown rapidly took off, staging as many as six meetings by the end of the century.

A gentleman wishing to become a member of the Leopardstown club was required to pay an annual subscription of 5 guineas, which entitled himself and two ladies to admission to the club enclosure, paddock and park and free admission for his carriage to the members' carriage enclosure. Rule III of the Leopardstown club stated that membership passes were not transferable. Any breach of this regulation would result in the offender being struck off the list. However, Rule IV allowed a certain amount of flexibility by stating that 'the ladies' passes are transferable,' although members obviously could not take too many liberties as the committee declared its power to remove the name of any member 'if it has been proved that he has misconducted himself'.

Whiffs of the controversy that had surrounded the opening of Leopardstown were to resurface eleven years later. Captain George Quin's circular 5-furlong track had created such antipathy amongst trainers, and probably their equine charges too, that Quin eventually relaid the track on the straight. From the outset the results on the new 5-furlong course were different, to say the very least. But nobody thought to question the distance until August 1897 when the winning time was recorded by Co. Dublin trainer F. F. McCabe as 56 seconds, more than 10 seconds faster than his filly Sabine Queen had recorded in a timed trial at home.

Down at the start the handler is left to walk the horse while the jockey goes through his riding orders. The handlers need to be quick thinking and fleet of foot themselves during the risky business of loading fractious Thoroughbreds into the starting stalls.

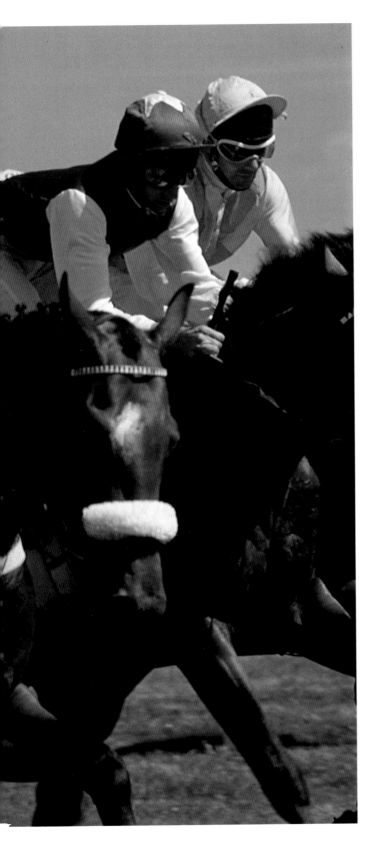

The course was measured and discovered to be well under the 5 furlongs it purported to be. Quin was fined £100 for this misdemeanour and was ordered to close the track. His third 5-furlong course was also a non-starter as it was declared impossible to view either the start or the finish from the stands. Racegoers were to wait until the new century before Leopardstown finally came up with the right answer.

By then Dublin had another metropolitan racecourse in the new Phoenix Park track, which was opened in August 1901, initially for flat meetings only. The design of the track was modelled directly on Hurst Park in England, but problems were to beset this course later in its life as well. The stands were positioned at such an angle to the track that it took a practised eye to judge the winner of a race. There was, reputedly, a spot somewhere in the stand, roughly the size of a single spectator, from where the results could be accurately gauged. The exact location of this spot remained a well kept secret, which was probably all to the good if untoward scenes were to be prevented from breaking out on the terraces.

Harry Peard, whose wife Fanny was involved in the administration of both the horse trials and showjumping circuits, had been one of the founders of the new track. The Park was closed down in 1982 when owner Patrick Gallagher declared himself bankrupt. But it reopened, following a complete facelift in 1983, when it was bought by a company headed by Vincent O'Brien and his associates. In spite of extensive modernization, costing around £5 million, the Park had lost much of its appeal to the people of Dublin.

Irish Californian Brian Sweeney was originally brought in to run the newly upholstered track, but personal problems left the post vacant and O'Brien approached Jonathan Irwin to take over. Irwin and later his partner John Sanderson, who had masterminded the success of York racecourse, were given a franchise to run the Park. With the introduction of what Irwin saw as 'top-class racing in front of the stands and a carnival behind', the people began to return to the Park, with attendances averaging 5,000 by the end of the decade.

The Park's launch of the spectacular Cartier Million in 1988, linked through Jonathan Irwin to the phenomenally successful yearling sale at Goffs run under the same exclusive banner, attracted ripples of excitement. Only the selected yearlings catalogued for this special sale twelve months previously could be entered for this valuable race, in which the winner took home £500,000.

The short-lived Cartier Million was the richest race for two-year-olds in Europe. The Park also ran the richest Group 1 two-year-old race in the Heinz 57 Stakes and hosted the prestigious Phoenix Champion Stakes. With this sort of *curriculum vitae* it came as an enormous shock to the racing fraternity, including Jonathan Irwin, when it was announced in September 1989 that the owners of the racecourse were

A level break as the runners in the Irish Derby get into their stride over the first furlong.

But other courses had suffered similar fates earlier in the century. Although the First World War initially posed no great threat to racing in Ireland, Fermoy racecourse in Co. Cork was acquired for military purposes in 1915 and was closed down. Two years later Cork Park was bought by Henry Ford, of motor vehicle fame, as the site for a new factory, which removed yet another southern track from the lists. The old strand racecourse at Tramore in Co. Waterford, which had been designed by Thomas Waters in 1870, had been reclaimed by the sea in 1912. The present-day course was built in 1917 to stem the tide of disappearing tracks in Munster, but although Tramore survived the crisis years of the late eighties it too has a dubious future.

In September of the previous year Tipperary town had added a new course and in 1924 another was opened at Mallow to make up for the loss of Cork Park. Naas also made its debut a month later. But by the beginning of the 1990s Ireland had lost nine tracks in just over half a century – Longford (1937), Miltown Malbay and Claremorris (1941), Rathkeale (1942), Mullacurry (1958), Mullingar (1967), Baldoyle (1972), Tuam (1974) and Phoenix Park (1990).

During the early years of the twentieth century racing was managing to keep pace with the times. The Curragh retained

RIGHT: *Jacqueline O'Brien is known in the racing world as the wife of Ireland's most famous trainer, Vincent O'Brien, but she is also established as a highly successful photographer in her own right.*

FAR RIGHT: *Former National Hunt jockey, turned trainer, turned television commentator, Ted Walsh discusses a point with fellow RTE commentator, Robert Hall.*

seeking planning permission to build a housing estate and luxury hotel complex on the site within the next two years. 'I can understand why the owners have done it,' said Irwin shortly after the bombshell dropped. 'It would have been remiss of their financial advisers if they hadn't suggested such a course of action. What people don't realise is that there are only two individuals [himself and John Sanderson] standing between Phoenix Park as a racecourse and it becoming a building site. We need the public's support.' That support was not forthcoming, however, and the final Cartier Million in October 1990 was the swansong of the Phoenix Park racecourse.

its role as the primary racecourse as well as the nerve centre of training in Ireland. Horses and sheep dominate the Curragh; although the sheep are only tolerated, prevented from straying too far by the judicious use of sheep grids, the horse is the king. Even in the twentieth century the traffic has to stop if a trainer wants to bring his string of Thoroughbreds across the main road. There is also a lollipop man stationed at the main crossing point to make sure that the multiple horse-power vehicles show the proper courtesy to their far more elegant predecessors.

But the stewards at the Curragh were at a loss to know what to do about a particular incident that occurred there not

long after the new century was born. Only three horses had been declared for a three-year-old race: the favourite, St Dunstan, ridden by John Doyle; Bell H, ridden by John Thompson; and Marble Hall, with Leslie Brabazon in the saddle, an uncle of the famous Aubrey Brabazon. The horses were actually under starter's orders when a hawk-eyed punter noticed that the favourite was listed on the card as a four-year-old and was therefore ineligible for the race. It was too late for him to do anything but put his money on one of the challengers.

Dunstan and Bell H disputed the race in the early stages and, approaching a bend, Thompson cut in to make up some

ground with Bell H. But the horse swerved and fell, hit its head on a stone post marking the bend and was killed instantly. Dunstan went on to win unopposed, but was immediately disqualified, leaving the race to the mercy of the only remaining runner Marble Hall. It was then discovered that, under the qualifications stated on the card, Marble Hall's jockey Leslie Brabazon was also ineligible. The qualifications stated that the race was open to 'jockeys with 5lbs extra and qualified riders under rule 96 (i) and (ii)'. It should have read, 'under rule 96 (i) or (ii)', but as Brabazon was not qualified under both he too was disqualified. The result? A three-horse race in which one horse was disqualified, one rider disqualified

An aerial shot of the Curragh on Irish Derby day. The serious racegoers are already on parade, but the fashion-conscious will wait until there is a better crowd to appreciate their arrival.

and one horse killed. There was nothing left to award the race to, so the stewards were given no choice but to pretend it had never happened.

Rather more recently the stewards were presented with the bizarre sight of a horse being given a lead by a pony, not over a fence, but at the start of a flat race. The horse apparently declined to start unless given the opportunity to set off in pursuit of its small companion.

One of the human stars on the post-World War I racing scene was Tommy Burns. Born in 1897 and known to all as The Scotsman, Tommy was the father of T. P. Burns, the man who rode the brilliant Ballymoss and the mare Gladness to so many victories as Vincent O'Brien's number one jockey between 1953 and 1959. It was the mare's victory that brought off what T.P. describes as 'one of the biggest Ballydoyle coups' in a maiden at Manchester. 'It was a very, very big gamble in the days when a pound really was a pound.' But although he would not be drawn into revealing how much money was made by the Ballydoyle inmates and friends in this spectacular bet, he admitted that he did not get too much extra for riding the means to produce these riches.

The starter at the Phoenix Park racecourse. Despite all attempts to save it, the Dublin track finally closed its gates in October 1990 after the last running of the Cartier Million.

T.P. was later taken in under the Ballydoyle umbrella when he became assistant trainer to Vincent O'Brien at the end of 1976. He remained in Tipperary until 1984 when he moved back to the Curragh to take on the same role with Dermot Weld.

Tommy Burns senior had travelled over to Ireland from his native Ayr in 1915 when his father James Burns had come to train for Colonel Hall-Walker, owner of the Tully Stud. When James Burns returned to Scotland in December 1918, Tommy stayed in Ireland because the English Jockey Club refused to give him a licence. His ability on a horse was legendary within the industry, and he was described by his contemporaries and his juniors as a perfect horseman and jockey. But in spite of the plaudits offered to him, Tommy always claimed his son was better. 'I was a good rider, but T.P. was one of the best jockeys I ever saw.'

Spry and animated right up to the time of his death only days after his 92nd birthday, Tommy Burns was not suffering from fading memory when he said he could not remember how many winners he rode in a career that spanned forty-three years, he simply declared that there were too many to count. Claiming twenty-one Irish Classics, Tommy recalled in a voice that still had a twang of the Scottish brogue about it, how he rode Upadee to beat Lester Piggott at Ascot in 1956. At the age of fifty-nine Burns then hung up his boots and, turning to training, produced Vimadee (out of his Ascot winner Upadee) to win the Irish St Leger in 1961, when ridden by his son T.P. to beat that year's Irish Derby winner, Your Highness.

As a lightweight jockey Tommy Burns was able to ride on the flat and over fences, although his chasing mounts were obviously well weighed down with lead. Millenium, his Metropolitan Chase winner at the old Ballydoyle racecourse in the early 1920s, was carrying 12st 7lb. That same day, Burns had won a two-year-old flat race with just 8st 4lb. That sort of versatility was shown to even greater effect by Martin Molony, Joe Canty and Ted Walsh, all of whom could do the weight to ride the winners of a flat race, a hurdle and a chase in the one day. Aubrey Brabazon, who was to step into Tommy Burns' not yet vacated shoes after the Second World War, was of a similar build to the Scotsman. Too light for chasing and just that bit too heavy for the flat, both he and Martin Molony weighed in at about 8st 10lb. Brabazon in fact was so light in his early days that he started riding as an amateur at the age of thirteen in 1934 and then reverted to being an apprentice as he could only tip the scales at 7st and amateurs were expected to carry 11st.

His hat-trick in the Cheltenham Gold Cup with Cottage Rake and double in the Champion Hurdle with Hatton's Grace are probably his most memorable performances. But Brabazon was equally gifted on the flat.

Phoenix Park was to play a major role in his career. He had his first ride there as an amateur in 1934 and, the following year, rode his first winner on the same track, bringing the Bob Fetherstonhaugh-trained Queen Christina home in front for Colonel Charles Loder, owner of the famous Pretty Polly. This victory earned Queen Christina's connections a mere £45. Brabazon also rode his first double at the Park and had his last ride there. And, in the previous generation, his father Cecil Brabazon had had his last winning ride at the Park. Cecil Brabazon, who remained an amateur throughout his race-riding career, won the Conyngham Cup in 1910 and went on to become leading trainer in 1940.

His son was much sought after to ride winners on the flat or over fences, even though the top jump horses would have to carry enormous quantities of lead to make up for Brabazon's spare frame. This nearly caused his undoing in the 1946 Liverpool Hurdle when Prince Toi was burdened with 12st 7lb. The horse put in an extravagant leap over the second last, well clear of the field. But this was long before the invention of the elasticated girth and, in the split second that the horse's muscles contracted in their mid-air stretch, the girth could not shrink with them. The saddle slipped round and Brabazon was unceremoniously dumped on the ground while the rest of the field galloped over him to contest the honours.

Two years later Brabazon hit the highlight of his flat career when he rode Masaka to win the Irish Oaks for the present Aga Khan's grandfather. The filly had already won the English equivalent with Billy Nevitt up and it was decided that, *en route* to her new career as a broodmare at Ballymany, she might as well go for the Irish Classic as well. Masaka duly obliged and Prince Aly was called upon to do the honours of leading her in as the Aga Khan was not racing that day. The smiling faces that filled the newspapers the following day were far from the truth, however, as a photograph that Aubrey Brabazon still treasures depicts all too clearly. The private picture shows a rather dejected looking Brabazon being roundly abused by Prince Aly, who not only owned the runner-up, Amina, but had a £500 bet on her to win. He told Brabazon in no uncertain terms what he thought of him and the filly who had conspired so blatantly to rob him of his big win, only just managing to turn on the charm in time as they entered the winner's enclosure.

Dermot Weld's stable jockey, Michael Kinane, rode his share of winners at Phoenix Park, including The Caretaker, winner of the 1989 Cartier Million in the same weekend that Kinane piloted Carroll House to victory in the Prix de l'Arc de Triomphe.

Brabazon, again unwittingly, was involved in another row some time later with the then champion jockey in England, Arthur 'Scobie' Breasley. On the first day of Ascot, Brabazon was being interviewed by Clive Graham, racing correspondent for *The Daily Express*. Graham was none too amused when one of the agency boys interrupted the interview to ask who was riding the favourite in the big race the following day. 'A.B. of course,' snapped Graham, momentarily breaking off from his interrogation of Brabazon. It came as a shock to more than just Brabazon when that evening's newspapers proclaimed in banner headlines that he would be aiming for victory on the ante-post favourite in the feature race the next afternoon.

'I decided I'd better watch what I ate that night so I would be able to do the weight,' declared Brabazon. 'But the next day Scobie Breasley was furious and asked me what the hell did I think I was doing pinching his rides. It was okay in the end when we realized what had happened. The young agency boy had thought that Clive Graham meant me when he said A.B., but of course he meant Scobie Breasley. Scobie went out and rode the horse. I can't remember if he won, but he was bloody annoyed about it at the time.'

In the year that Europe entered her second major confrontation of the century, Joe McGrath, who had founded the Irish Hospital Sweepstakes, bought Windsor Slipper who became the second winner of the Irish Triple Crown when ridden by the great Morny Wing, champion jockey in both 1941 and 1942. Windsor Slipper was retired to stand at McGrath's Brownstown Stud, which also housed the first winner of the Irish Triple Crown, the colt Museum who was ridden in two of his Classic races by Steve Donoghue (with whom T. P. Burns served part of his apprenticeship) and in the 2,000 Guineas by Martin Quirke.

Joe McGrath was to be leading owner in Ireland for five successive years between 1942 and 1946 and it was during that period that Major Dermot McCalmont also came to the fore, winning the Irish Derby in 1944 with Slide On and the following year with Piccadilly. He also won the 1944 Irish Oaks with Avoca and was made a steward of the Turf Club. All three of his Classic winners of that era were ridden by Jack Moylan, whose grandson Pat Eddery has since dominated international racing.

Two characters who were to be seen at virtually every race meeting in the late 1940s and early 1950s were Twinny Byrne and Buckets Moloney. Twinny features in literally hundreds of pictures of horses being led in after winning and was the bane of the press photographers' lives. Regardless of who the winning owner was Twinny would latch on to the other side of the horse and would, invariably, be on the side nearest the camera, frequently managing to obscure the intended subject of the photograph. It is easy to imagine the curses that would escape the lips of the boys in the darkroom as the prints gradually developed in their chemical baths to reveal Twinny's familiar face yet again.

Buckets Moloney was a rotund character who originally earned his crust doing the rounds with a sponge and bucket of water for the bookies to wipe the prices for the previous race off their boards. Buckets was a permanent fixture at all the race meetings. He eventually got rather too grand for such a menial task and dispensed with his bucket, but the nickname stuck with him to the end. Though neither encroached on the other's territory, Twinny and Buckets had a mutual disrespect for each other.

Another familiar face who, unlike Twinny and Buckets, was very much a part of the establishment hierarchy in his capacity as Turf Club vet during the 1980s, is Richard Teevan. On one particular occasion he had arranged to leave tickets for a friend on the gate at the Curragh. The friend arrived and inquired of the gateman whether Mr Teevan had left the tickets for him as arranged. 'Mr Teevan, don't know any Mr Teevan,' came the gruff response from a gateman obviously not over enamoured with his job. 'Of course you do, he's the Turf Club vet,' said the exasperated friend, envisaging his day's racing being spent arguing with a cantankerous white-coated official. Recognition dawned slowly on the man's face as the punter went on with his description. 'The short, fat, baldy man with the red face,' he said, his loyalty to his friend evaporating once his goal was in sight. Teevan tells this story against himself, even though it is hardly complimentary and, indeed, a long way from the truth. He has since been elevated to even higher stations, now labouring under the unwieldy title of Senior Stewards' Secretary. Woe betide anyone who describes him as a short, fat, baldy man with a red face now!

Liam Ward, the six times champion jockey who is the only one of his calling to have been made a steward of the Turf Club since retiring, remembers a day when some of his predecessors did him no favours. Ballet Royal, a horse trained by the great gambling man Tommy O'Brien in the 1960s, was 20 yards short of the winning post and clear of the field at the Curragh when he suddenly shied, for no apparent reason (and it was certainly well before the infamous stun gun had been heard of), dumping his jockey Gerry Cooney. O'Brien, owner of a mine in Ballingarry down in Tipperary and known as Tommy Coal, was notorious for the massive bets he would lay on his horses. Cooney was promptly sacked and Liam Ward called in to take the ride on Ballet Royal in his next race at Phoenix Park.

The horse was badly hampered in the final stages, but Ward did not bother to object, knowing that justice would be done in the resulting stewards' enquiry. The patrol film of the race was minutely examined by the august bodies, but it failed to show the side of the track where the incident had occurred and once again Ballet Royal was robbed of his rightful victory.

Returning to the Curragh, the horse veered across the track on the run in to lose yet again. But his final race at Leopardstown was even more dramatic. Ward had him out in front 20 yards from the line when one of Ballet Royal's front legs suddenly snapped. Another victory gone and this time the horse was gone too. Tommy Coal reckoned the horse had cost him at least £60,000 in bets and his original purchase price.

As the 1970s came to a close the Aga Khan's mare Sharmeen, by Val de Loir, produced a white-faced bay colt that was to take the international press by storm, both on and off the racecourse. Shergar, a 1978 son of Great Nephew, was bred at the Aga Khan's Sheshoon Stud on the Curragh. Trained by Michael Stoute at Newmarket, the colt won the Kris Plate at Newbury on his two-year-old debut in 1980. Having confirmed his trainer's belief that this was a very promising youngster, Shergar was then upped a grade and came out next in a tough Group 1 race, the William Hill Futurity Stakes in which he finished a good second to Beldale Flutter.

Shergar was to become racehorse of the year in 1981. He started the season with a 10-length victory in the Guardian Newspaper Classic Trial at Sandown and he then blitzed the opposition when winning the Chester Vase by 12 lengths. But it was his phenomenal burst of speed in the Epsom Derby of that year that marked him down as something special. Ridden by the nineteen-year-old Walter Swinburn, Shergar went into overdrive to finish 10 lengths clear of Glint of Gold.

The Aga Khan's superstar then returned to the land of his birth where he added the Irish Sweeps Derby to his tally, holding off Cut Above (the only horse to beat him that year) by 4 lengths. He claimed the King George VI Stakes by a similar distance shortly afterwards. In his six races as a three-year-old, Shergar was beaten only in the last, his amazing speed proving his undoing over the longer distance in the St Leger where he went down by a dozen lengths, finishing fourth to Cut Above.

The colt was then retired to stand at the Aga Khan's Ballymany Stud, having been syndicated for £10 million. The forty shares were sold at £250,000 apiece, with the Aga Khan retaining seven units. In his first season at stud, Shergar covered forty-two mares, forty of which went in foal. His stud fee was £70,000, half of which was payable on covering with the balance falling due on 1 October if the mare was tested in foal.

But, before he had a chance to embark on his second season and before any of his first crop of foals were on the ground, Shergar was kidnapped in one of the most dramatic incidents ever to hit the Irish bloodstock industry. At approximately 8.30 p.m. on Tuesday, 8 February 1983 (a week before the start of the covering season), a gang of five armed and masked men forced stud groom John Fitzgerald to identify Shergar and then help load him into a grey two-horse trailer. Since that moment nothing has been seen of the dual Derby winner.

Mrs Fitzgerald and five of her seven children were held at gunpoint during the theft and then locked into a room in their house. While the gang leaders made their getaway with the horse, John Fitzgerald was driven in a van, lying face downwards, to Kilcock, about 20 miles away from Ballymany, where he was released. The police were alerted at 5 a.m. on the morning of Wednesday, 9 February.

The gang's original demand of a £2 million ransom met with no response from the shareholders, as the Irish police combed the countryside in their searches for the horse. But, in response to an anonymous phone call, three British racing journalists, Lord Oaksey from the BBC, Derek Thompson of ITV and Peter Campling from *The Sun*, were flown to Belfast to act as intermediaries. The Co. Down trainer Jeremy Maxwell and his wife Judy were also brought in to assist with the negotiations, while Chief Superintendent Jim Murphy of the Garda Siochana led the investigations in the south.

The Sporting Life offered a £10,000 reward for the safe return of Shergar and Captain Sean Berry of the Irish Thoroughbred Breeders Association (ITBA) also promised what was termed 'a substantial reward', stating at the time, 'I don't think the Irish mentality would lend itself to doing anything to harm the horse'.

Having drawn a blank in the north of Ireland, the search was then concentrated on the Republic. Several anonymous phone calls were received claiming that Shergar had injured himself and been put down, but none of these were verified.

The then Fianna Fail leader Charles Haughey called on the Minister for Justice to provide protection for the major stud farms: 'There is a very large overseas investment in these stud farms and at this time of the year there are many valuable mares from abroad in this country visiting Irish stallions.' As negotiations through a London intermediary for a £1 million reward continued, some of the fifty-five mares booked for Shergar started to arrive at Ballymany, including the 1,000 Guineas winner On The House and the winner of the Arc, Akiyda.

But the only news of the horse came from the untraceable phone calls to the BBC and the *Belfast Newsletter* which claimed that the horse had been transported to stand at stud in the Middle East. The caller stated that earlier reports claiming that the horse was dead were in fact coded messages to indicate that the horse had been successfully exported to the Middle East. These claims were refuted by several bloodstock transport agencies who stated that it would have been impossible to either ship or fly the horse out of the country

By the start of the big race any vantage point will do to get a good view of the action. It is not unknown for the desperate few, with a good head for heights, to perch on the roof of the stands.

without a veterinary inspection, advance booking and documents signed by the Department of Agriculture.

On 22 February Kildare County Council confirmed that it had received a claim for £20 million from the shareholders under the Malicious Injuries Act. The Irish Farmers Association mounted a two-day countrywide search through its 100,000 members and the ITBA opened a hot-line for information regarding the case.

It is said that £750,000 was paid out in used bank notes from the boot of a car in Co. Clare. Having received his pay-off the self-styled kidnapper then vanished as conclusively as his supposed victim had done, leaving two leading members of the bloodstock industry considerably poorer and painfully aware of how easily they had been duped.

Eight weeks after the kidnapping there were further rumours that an even more substantial ransom of £1.5 million had been paid. But there was still no sign of Shergar and, on 9 May, the ninety-day deadline for shareholders to submit their insurance claim to Lloyds expired. Just over a month later Lloyds declared Shergar dead and agreed to pay out £7 million sterling to shareholders who had insured their interests for theft, not death. It was the largest payout that had ever been made in the history of bloodstock insurance.

Theories abound as to what happened to Shergar, but there seems no doubt that the horse is no longer alive. Fears that the kidnapping would have a detrimental effect on the breeding industry, with foreign owners unwilling to risk their valuable stallions or mares in Ireland, thankfully proved unfounded,

possibly because of the low VAT rate on bloodstock in Ireland. The European Single Market could not alter this as the EC had already agreed in September 1991 that the Irish VAT rate of 2.3 per cent on bloodstock would remain, although that is to be reviewed in 1996. This figure compares very favourably with the rest of Europe, particularly Britain where bloodstock is taxable at a rate of 17.5 per cent. Even posthumously, Shergar did his bit for the Irish bloodstock industry, helping to save the apparently stricken sales figures in 1984 when a yearling son of his was sold at Goffs for £3.2 million, still a European record for a yearling. Named Authaal, he went on to win the 1986 Irish St Leger.

The 1980s will also be remembered for the silent but very public tussle between the acknowledged rulers of the flat kingdom, owner Robert Sangster and legendary trainer Vincent O'Brien, and the new pretenders to the throne, the Maktoums, the royal family of Dubai. The public battles were on the racecourses of Europe. Playing to a rather more intimate but infinitely more knowledgeable gallery were the scenes enacted at the major sales complexes, particularly the July yearling sales at Keeneland where the previously bottomless Sangster/O'Brien cheque book finally met its match, but not before it had been used to pay a world record price of $13.1 million for a son of Nijinsky, Seattle Dancer, in 1985.

The Maktoums, in dazzling displays of wealth which represented mere pocket money to the oil-rich sheikhs, could apparently outbid everyone who cared to take them on. Sangster and O'Brien were the only ones who tried and, in most cases, found themselves short of ammunition. There were triumphs in both camps. And there were the disasters that the rival faction could gloat over, most notably the Maktoums' purchase of Snaafi Dancer in 1982 for the then record sum of $10.2 million. The horse never appeared on a racecourse and was retired to an equally unsuccessful career at stud.

But the warfare left a trail of devastation in its wake as the less monied members of an already cut-throat business reeled and, in many cases, collapsed under the burden of massively spiralling prices against which they simply could not compete. The lower end of the sport and the industry is still suffering, although the plea from the racing industry for some return for the vast sums it pours into the Government's coffers finally paid dividends when it was announced in 1990 that a Government grant of £3 million per annum would be issued jointly to horse and greyhound racing with bloodstock eligible for £2½ million of this. The grant was aimed at increasing the minimum level of prize-money and improving the marketing of bloodstock at home and abroad.

Although this funding was welcomed by the racing industry, it had been hoped that the Government would agree to give racing a percentage of monies raised through off-course betting rather than the fixed sum agreed in the grant. The industry is worth, at a conservative estimate, £40 million a year. It generates a further £300 million in bets, two-thirds of which are laid off-course and therefore escape the 5 per cent levy which is fed directly back into the industry to finance the Racing Board. This levy was introduced in 1945 with the formation of the Racing Board. Prior to 1926 the only strictly legal form of betting was at race meetings, but when off-course betting was legalized the Government instantly slapped a 5 per cent tax on it, with on-course betting taxed at $2\frac{1}{2}$ per cent. A moratorium on tax prevailed from 1931 until 1945 when the Racing Board came into being. Its 5 per cent levy was halved the following year. In 1964 the levy returned to its original 5 per cent following the introduction of a $2\frac{1}{2}$ per cent turnover tax by the State.

This new tax applied to both on- and off-course betting, but was subsequently removed from on-course betting following objections from the Racing Board. However, this was only on the understanding that the Board would increase its levy by $2\frac{1}{2}$ per cent. The Government reintroduced taxation on on-course betting in 1980 when the levy was increased to $7\frac{1}{2}$ per cent, to include State tax of $1\frac{1}{2}$ per cent. But, appropriately enough on April Fool's Day of 1985, the levy was once again pitched at 5 per cent, the Government renouncing all claims on this income.

Tax on off-course betting has also swung up and down the percentage scale, hitting 20 per cent in 1975. This merely resulted in a proliferation of illegal betting and greatly increased income for the British bookies who accepted telephone bets from their beleaguered Irish cousins. As a result the Government brought the level of taxation back down to 10 per cent in 1985, initially for a trial period. But although the announcement of the Government grant raised morale in 1990 there is no doubt that the industry would be better served by a share in the off-course betting revenue. The big fixtures such as the Galway Festival meeting in July, the riotous week in Listowel in September and the Christmas meeting at Leopardstown all continue to prosper. But even the high profile tracks are having their difficulties and one false move can bring about disaster.

Surely an industry that generates so much in terms of income, employment and enjoyment, deserves a slice of its own profits. Ireland is the only racing nation in the world whose Government does not return a share of the off-course betting to the racing authorities in one form or another. The punters who support racing only from the inside of their local bookies are doing the sport a huge disservice. A share in that vast income still remains beyond the reach of the very industry that creates it.

The gloom of the recession was lightened by the

appearance at the beginning of the nineties of two Irish-breds that captured the imagination of the racing press and public alike. In the first year of the decade the filly Salsabil, winner of the English 1,000 Guineas and the Oaks, took on the colts at the Curragh to win the Irish Derby ridden out hands and heels by Willie Carson. Hamdan Al Maktoum named the filly that he had bought for 400,000 guineas at the Highflyer Sales in Newmarket after one of the rivers in heaven mentioned in the Koran.

After Salsabil's English wins, Coolmore's John Magnier sent a congratulatory telegram to the filly's trainer John Dunlop suggesting Salsabil should be entered in the Irish Derby. Her owner had no hesitation in paying out the £60,000 supplementary fee for a late entry and the filly returned to her native land where, in front of the packed stands at the Curragh, she hit the front at the furlong pole and was never caught to become the first filly to win both the Oaks and the Irish Derby since 1900.

Salsabil was bred by Pat O'Kelly at Kilcarn Stud, just outside Navan in Co. Meath. Her dam, Flame of Tara (by Artaius), had been retained by her owner and sent into training with Jim Bolger to win the Coronation Stakes at Ascot. Pat O'Kelly turned down an offer of several million for the mare from the Muslim sheikh who ended up buying her second foal instead. Flame of Tara's first foal was the good filly Nearctic Flame, but it was Salsabil that made Pat O'Kelly realize what a wise decision she had made in turning down Hamdan Al Maktoum's millions for the mare.

Freelancer Kevin Manning, a former champion apprentice when riding for Jim Bolger, mentally prepares himself for the task ahead.

Father Michael Cleary, a well-known Dublin priest, at the Nun Run at Trim. The riders in this annual race have all genuinely taken holy orders, as opposed to mere riding orders.

Tony O'Reilly, former Irish international rugby player and now managing director and chief executive of the Heinz corporation, is a great supporter of Irish racing.

Flame of Tara's third foal, Marju, was second in the 1991 English Derby to a flashy chestnut colt with a flaxen mane and tail that was to provide yet another boost for Irish breeding. This was Generous, the Caerleon colt bred by David and Diane Nagle at Barronstown Stud in Grangecon, Co. Wicklow. The dam was Doff the Derby, a half sister to Trillion who produced Triptych, the Irish 2,000 Guineas winner. Generous came under the hammer at Goffs as a foal and was sold for 80,000 guineas. The colt returned to the Co. Kildare sales ring as a yearling and was knocked down to Anthony Penfold, racing manager for Khaled Abdulla, for a mere 200,000 guineas. The chestnut's flashy looks went against him, but Penfold knew that he had got a superbly made colt.

Generous had been bought for Prince Fahd Salman, the nephew and son-in-law of Khaled Abdulla, and the newly purchased yearling was sent into training with Paul Cole. Having won the Coventry Stakes at Ascot in his first season Generous disappointed in his next few races. But he proved himself to be a real fighter, battling through the mud to win the Group 1 Dewhurst Stakes at the end of his two-year-old career. Generous could only manage fourth place in the 1991 2,000 Guineas and it was not until the colt got his nose home first in the Epsom Derby that the racing press renewed its interest in him. Generous then added the King George and Queen Elizabeth Diamond Stakes to his tally before returning to Ireland to win the Irish Derby, beating the French Derby winner Suave Dancer in the process. His final outing was at Longchamp in the Arc before he was retired to stand at Banstead Manor, Khaled Abdulla's English stud.

CHAPTER FIVE

TRAINERS AND JOCKEYS

*A*WAY WITH HORSES, the ability to make them perform to the very best of their capability, is an integral part of the Irish character. In the world of the Thoroughbred, one man seems to possess an extra touch of magic, that flair which can only be described as genius. Vincent O'Brien's tally of winners, both on the flat and over fences, has made his a name to be regarded with trepidation by his rivals and sheer admiration by his supporters.

O'Brien produced three consecutive winners of the Aintree Grand National in the years 1953 to 1955 with Early Mist, Royal Tan and Quare Times. He also recorded two more remarkable hat-tricks in the Cheltenham Gold Cup and Champion Hurdle, with Cottage Rake coming home in front to claim the Gold Cup in 1948, 1949 and 1950 and Hatton's Grace achieving a similar feat with his three successive victories in the Champion Hurdle between 1949 and 1951. Knock Hard then went on to give the Cork-born trainer his

fourth Gold Cup in 1953 and, in the meantime, Alberoni won the Irish Grand National in 1952.

But the switch to the flat proved even more successful. Chamier's win in the 1953 Irish Derby was the start of an era that was to bring O'Brien six Epsom Derbys, four further wins in the Irish equivalent, a quartet of victories in both the English and Irish 2,000 Guineas amongst a list of Classic successes that also includes the 1977/78 double in the Prix de l'Arc de Triomphe by Alleged to add to Ballymoss' win in 1958 plus Sir Ivor's shattering of the opposition in America's Washington International in 1968.

Vincent O'Brien was born on 9 April 1917 in Churchtown, Co. Cork, within hacking distance of Buttevant where the first recorded steeplechase had been run 165 years previously *en route* to the church in Doneraile. Interestingly, Churchtown was also the site of a horse fair where, reputedly, Napoleon's favourite horse Marengo was bought. The first son of Dan

---

OPPOSITE: The final tune-up before the big race. ABOVE: *Dermot Weld faces the press.*

O'Brien's second family, Vincent was surrounded by horses from an early age and remembers reciting horses' pedigrees on his father's knee at the age of three. Although Dan O'Brien trained point-to-pointers on a small scale, he was not to know that in his son he had produced a child who was to become recognized worldwide as the king of trainers.

Having persuaded his father to allow him to leave school shortly before his fifteenth birthday, Vincent then spent a year training with Fred Clarke at Leopardstown racecourse just outside Dublin. Then, the following year, he was granted an amateur rider's permit to ride under both Rules. But it was not until November 1940 that Vincent rode his first winner, bringing his father's Hallowment home ahead of the field in a bumper (amateur flat race) at Limerick.

In the spring of 1941 Vincent was schooling his father's mare White Squirrel for the coming point-to-points, but the entire season was cancelled due to an outbreak of foot-and-mouth disease. Not to be thwarted, Vincent started working

The horsewalker allows manpower to be deployed elsewhere while the horse is cooled off after exercise.

the mare with some of the flat horses and, discovering her to be more than capable of producing the extra speed demanded of her, he entered White Squirrel for a race at Clonmel. The mare duly went ahead and won the race, with Vincent in the saddle, at a price of 10/1 which earned the impoverished Vincent 'a good bit of money' for his £4 stake, although his father was luckier, as he had been able to get odds of 20/1 and put £10 on White Squirrel to win.

Two years later Dan O'Brien was dead and the farm was made over to Vincent's half-brother in the will. Luckily, for Irish racing history at least, he had no interest in horses and rented the yard and gallops to Vincent who promptly set about looking for owners willing to send their horses to him. His first owner was the Dublin-based but Gloucestershire-born wool-broker Frank Vickerman, who was to run his horses under the name D. G. B. O'Brien. That year, 1943, he put a couple of horses into training with Vincent and, twelve

months later, managed to recoup £5,000 through two other horses in the yard, Drybob and the appropriately named Good Days. With odds of 800/1 against completing the double, Drybob dead-heated for the Irish Cambridgeshire and Good Days won the Irish Cesarewitch. Although Drybob's shared victory halved their winnings, it was a coup that started O'Brien and Vickerman off on a trail of success.

But it was the horse Cottage Rake that was to bring international fame to the young trainer. Brought to O'Brien's Churchtown yard literally from a bog at the age of five, Cottage Rake went on to produce the speed to win the Naas November Handicap and the 2-mile Irish Cesarewitch as well as the jumping ability to claim the Leopardstown Chase, three successive Cheltenham Gold Cups and the King George VI Chase at Kempton Park in an illustrious career that spanned eight seasons. Bred in Co. Cork, Cottage Rake is rated by his trainer as one of the century's best chasers, on a par with the wonder horse Arkle. Apart from being teamed up with the man who was to become one of the world's best producers of racehorses, Cottage Rake was partnered in his races by two very important figures in the Irish racing world, P. P. Hogan, who was one of the top amateur riders of the day and who went on to become arguably the country's most successful point-to-point trainer, and the brilliant Aubrey Brabazon, who rode The Rake in each of his three Gold Cup wins between 1948 and 1950.

It was Aubrey Brabazon who had given Vincent O'Brien his first win as a trainer, with Oversway in a 1943 flat race at Limerick Junction, over the hurdles with Wren Boy, also at the Junction seventeen months later and, finally, in June 1945, O'Brien's first success on a chase course, with Panay at Thurles. Brabazon would also have ridden O'Brien's first Irish Derby winner, Chamier in 1953, but a fall with his best known partner Cottage Rake at Hurst Park had resulted in a broken arm and robbed Brabazon of this accolade. His friend Billy Rickerby, a first cousin to Lester Piggott, was given the ride at the Curragh, but Chamier's owner Frank Vickerman said that if the horse won he would give Brabazon the same present as the jockey. After an objection Chamier was awarded the race and Vickerman was as good as his word.

Brabazon was given another gift after winning the second of Cottage Rake's Gold Cups at Cheltenham. This present was also totally unexpected. It came from Major Stirling-Stuart, owner of Cool Customer, a horse that Brabazon had steered to victory on numerous occasions. But on this particular occasion, Brabazon and Cottage Rake, in what the jockey describes as 'the hardest race the horse ever got', had proved the undoing of Cool Customer, wearing down his reserves to just pip him on the run in. Ironically, the Major had tried to buy Cottage Rake three years earlier, but the horse had been turned down for his wind. Nevertheless, as Cottage Rake and his acolytes stood in the winner's unsaddling enclosure at Cheltenham, the beaten owner quietly came through the throng, patted Cottage Rake and handed Brabazon a pair of cuff-links with Cool Customer's name and Brabazon's initials engraved on them.

Overlapping The Rake's Gold Cup hat-trick was another remarkable Cheltenham treble by the O'Brien stable, the three successive Champion Hurdle wins between 1949 and 1951 by Hatton's Grace with the brilliant Aubrey Brabazon in the saddle for the first two victories and Tim Moloney taking the ride in 1951. (Moloney also rode the French horse Sir Ken to win the Hurdle in 1952, 1953 and 1954 and was champion NH jockey in England five times.) Brabazon missed out on the Hatton's Grace treble because he had a retainer to ride for Clifford Nicholson and, since Nicholson had a runner in the 1951 Hurdle, AB was called in to ride it. Brabazon's horse for the day was Average but, not quite up to Champion Hurdle standard, he could only finish fifth.

These two major coups in Cheltenham's most prestigious races by a previously unheard of trainer from Ireland set the alarm bells ringing in the English racing scene. This young O'Brien was obviously a man to be taken seriously, someone who posed more than just a threat to the supremacy the British trainers had enjoyed over their own racing world for so long.

But this was only the beginning. O'Brien headed the English National Hunt trainers in 1953 with winnings totalling £15,515 and also became the first trainer to claim the Cheltenham Gold Cup, the Grand National at Aintree and the Irish Derby all in the same year. This was the year of O'Brien's first National win, although the English trainers could gain some measure of compensation from the fact that Early Mist was English, not Irish-bred, having been sold to Ireland as a yearling at the Newmarket sales in 1946.

Bryan Marshall was the jockey that steered Early Mist to that 1953 victory and, the following year, Marshall and

Vincent O'Brien uses the covered ring at Ballydoyle to check on the string and decide on each horse's programme before they head out to the gallops.

O'Brien teamed up again, although this time the third member of the trio was changed. This was the Co. Tipperary-bred Royal Tan, owned by Mrs Keogh who also had the triple Champion Hurdle winner Hatton's Grace and the 1953 Cheltenham Gold Cup victor Knock Hard.

O'Brien had four runners in the 1955 race, but it was neither of his two earlier winners who took the honours, nor Oriental Way ridden by Fred Winter. Bred in Thurles, Co. Tipperary, Quare Times (who the English commentators used to call Quaray Timees thinking the name was a Latin one) had

won his first race with Bryan Marshall in the saddle. But it was Pat Taaffe who rode him on his Aintree debut, which he made a winning one, sprinting home 12 lengths clear of the 1954 runner-up Tudor Line, to score Vincent O'Brien's famous hat-trick and lead home five Irish horses in the first six. And it was a good year for Pat Taaffe too, as he added the Prince of Wales Plate at Punchestown to his tally and also rode Umm to win both the Irish Grand National and the Galway Plate.

Four years later O'Brien gave up his National Hunt interests to concentrate on the more lucrative world of the

Each horse's state of fitness is carefully monitored by Vincent O'Brien at Ballydoyle.

flat. By then he was well established in his new home at Ballydoyle, near Cashel in Co. Tipperary. At the end of Cheltenham week in 1951 he had transferred his whole operation to this beautiful part of Ireland, surrounded by the Galtee mountains, the Knockmealdowns and the Comeraghs, with the stunning Slievenamon towering over them all. The Georgian farmhouse and 200 acres had been bought for £17,000, money raised through a run of successful bets and a bank loan. O'Brien's first job was to make gaps in the fences between the fields for the horses to work. Since most of the fields were separated by enormous banks with stone wall facings and hedges on top this was no easy task, but it was the start of what has now become 3 miles of superb gallops on grass, all-weather and sand surfaces. Ballydoyle now boasts 600 acres and a staff of eighty-five. There are three yards, a vet station, an isolation unit, barns for exercising in during bad weather and a covered ring where the trainer can make his initial checks on horses before they go out onto the gallops.

In 1954 O'Brien had his first brush with the authorities

when he was suspended for three months because of the inconsistent running of four of his horses. But this was of little significance compared to the serious allegations of drugging Chamour in the Ballysax Maiden Plate at the Curragh in April 1960 which resulted in an eighteen-month suspension that was later commuted to twelve months. O'Brien was not prepared to allow his reputation to become tarnished, however, and immediately sued the stewards of the Turf club for libel following the publication in the *Racing Calendar* of their findings.

In a High Court settlement O'Brien agreed to accept the stewards' statement that 'there was no evidence to suggest that he was either personally responsible for, or in any way an accessory to, the drugging of the colt, Chamour.' O'Brien felt that he had been vindicated by the statement and agreed to forgo any claim to damages.

It was in the September of 1955 that O'Brien first met American millionaire John McShain at the Tattersalls' sales in Doncaster. McShain asked O'Brien to buy some yearlings for him which he would then take straight back to the States to go into training. The horses were duly bought, but O'Brien managed to persuade the American to let him take the youngsters back to Ballydoyle and train them there. Included in this batch of yearlings was Ballymoss, the horse that was to win the Irish Derby, the St Leger, the King George VI and Queen Elizabeth Diamond Stakes at Ascot and the Prix de l'Arc de Triomphe. His first win came at Leopardstown in the September of 1956, a success which prompted O'Brien to write to his American patron and suggest that the horse should stay in training in Ireland and be aimed for the Epsom Derby the following May.

The horse's hatred of soft ground, which resulted in him being withdrawn from some top races at the last minute, may have driven the punters to distraction, but it allowed the year-older filly Gladness the opportunity to show her brilliance on the heavier going which she infinitely preferred. After a year of setbacks, Gladness finally appeared in a maiden plate at Manchester where, in a field of thirty runners, she trotted up to earn her connections more than just pocket money.

The following year Ballymoss finished a close second to Crepello at Epsom, but headed the field in the Irish Derby at the Curragh less than a month later. He then added the St Leger to his tally, but it was 1958 that was to be the glorious year when Ballymoss and Gladness between them claimed the Coronation Cup at Epsom, the Ascot Gold Cup, the Eclipse, the King George VI and Queen Elizabeth Diamond Stakes, the Goodwood Cup, the Ebor at York and the Prix de l'Arc, having teamed up with two new jockeys, Scobie Breasley for Ballymoss and Lester Piggott for the mare.

In that same year O'Brien went to the Keeneland sales where he was to meet another rich American, Raymond Guest, who was to own Vincent's first Epsom Derby winner,

Larkspur. The yearling colt by Never Say Die was bought at the Ballsbridge sales in Dublin for 12,200 guineas, but in 1962 he gave Vincent O'Brien his first Classic win outside Ireland. Raymond Guest also owned Sir Ivor, who won at Epsom six years later and who is in O'Brien's list of top four horses, the others being Nijinsky, El Gran Senor and Alleged.

The great Nijinsky, which Lester Piggott credited as being 'on his day, the most brilliant horse I've ever ridden', was owned by another American, Charles Engelhard, and was to start O'Brien's switch to American-bred horses, particularly the Northern Dancer lines. American-breds perhaps should not feature in a book on the Irish horse, but they are part of the success story that is Vincent O'Brien.

A spectacularly difficult horse to train, Nijinsky nevertheless won every race he ran in, except the last two. But it was in the 1970 season that he really came into his own, winning the Triple Crown (the 2,000 Guineas, the Derby and the St Leger), the Gladness Stakes and the Irish Derby at the Curragh, as well as the King George VI and Queen Elizabeth Diamond Stakes. His two defeats came in the Arc and the Champion Stakes at Newmarket where he was to finish second. Immediately afterwards the horse was syndicated for $5\frac{1}{2}$ million to stand at stud in America.

Another American colt, Roberto, was to give O'Brien his fourth Epsom Derby and Lester Piggott his sixth. Having won his first three outings at the Curragh in 1971, he finished a disappointing fourth when teamed up with Piggott for the Grand Criterium at Longchamp. In 1972 Roberto added the Phoenix Park Vauxhall Trial Stakes, the Epsom Derby and the Benson and Hedges Gold Cup at York to his tally, coming out the following season to finish second in the Nijinsky Stakes at Leopardstown before winning the Coronation Stakes at Epsom. On poor ground the horse was withdrawn from the Eclipse and then ran desperately badly at Ascot shortly afterwards. But during his preparation for the Champion Stakes, the leg trouble that had always been lurking under the surface flared up and Roberto was retired to stud.

It was in 1973 that the phenomenally successful partnership between O'Brien and Robert Sangster was forged. The pair came together when Vincent decided to buy into Tim Vigors' Coolmore Stud, on the other side of Fethard from Ballydoyle. Sangster, who had been looking for someone to train his horses for him, came in as a partner on the deal. John Magnier, who was to marry Vincent and Jacqueline's daughter Susan, then became the third member of a triumvirate that was to prove an unstoppable force in the Thoroughbred world. Coolmore and Magnier's Castle Hyde were amalgamated to form the beginning of a breeding empire that remains unrivalled in Europe.

O'Brien's 1977 Derby winner, The Minstrel, was another son of the prolific Northern Dancer, sire of the great Nijinsky,

No applause from the stands this time but, barring accidents, all these horses should make it to the racecourse, even if they never reach the exalted heights of the Curragh itself.

but was a totally different model, growing to just under 15.3 hands high at maturity. He won his three outings as a two-year-old, including the Larkspur Stakes at Leopardstown, and kept up the 100 per cent strike rate on his first appearance the following season. Beaten in both the English and Irish 2,000 Guineas, the little chestnut nevertheless managed to come up with the goods at Epsom, returned to Ireland to win the Irish Derby just over three weeks later and then added the King George and Queen Elizabeth Diamond Stakes by the narrowest of margins before being retired to stand at stud in Maryland.

Alleged, bought by Robert Sangster as a two-year-old in California, won the Prix de l'Arc de Triomphe at the end of his three-year-old career and, in spite of setbacks in 1978, won his three outings, including a second Arc. He suffered only one defeat during his racing career, at the hands of the Queen's filly Dunfermline who got up to beat him on the line for the 1977 St Leger. Alleged was then syndicated for $13 million.

Golden Fleece will always be remembered as O'Brien's 1982 Derby winner who died tragically early after only eighteen months at stud. Epsom was his fourth and last appearance on a racetrack and he remained unbeaten, setting a time in the Derby of 2 minutes 34.27 seconds, the fastest recorded since electrical timing had been brought in eighteen years earlier.

Vincent's son David was about to break into the big time, producing Robert Sangster's colt Assert to win both the French and Irish Derbys. Both Assert and Golden Fleece were syndicated at the end of that year for $24 million. Golden Fleece was retained to stand at Coolmore but, after just one season at stud, was stricken with stomach cancer from which he never recovered.

The main road south bisects the Curragh, but it is a familiar sight to see the traffic stopped to allow a string of horses to cross over on their way to and from the gallops.

David O'Brien was to hit the headlines again in 1984 when Secreto beat Vincent's great Derby hope El Gran Senor in a photo-finish, effectively destroying El Gran Senor's unbeaten record. But Vincent was to come out fighting again, underlying his belief in the statement, 'If I were to voice a philosophy I'd probably say I prefer to leave yesterday and get cracking with today.'

In the autumn of 1987 an entirely new concept in horse ownership was launched onto the Irish bloodstock scene with the flotation on the Stock Exchange of Classic Thoroughbreds PLC. It was the first opportunity for the small man to own a part share in a racehorse trained by Vincent O'Brien and, not surprisingly, shares were snapped up at the offer price of 30 pence on 22 October of that year. The 2,500 shareholders invested £15 million in the company chaired by O'Brien, who personally invested £1.5 million as well as his expertise to buy thirty-eight yearlings to go into training at Ballydoyle. With the exception of Royal Academy, the Classic Thoroughbreds purchases proved disappointing in the extreme, resulting in share prices plummeting from 28 pence to 16 pence in one black day in 1989 and dropping to an all-time low of 3 pence the following year.

Royal Academy was viewed as the potential saviour of Classic Thoroughbreds and his purchase price of $3½ million suggested that O'Brien had great faith in the youngster. His victory in the July Cup at Newmarket in 1990 previewed a dramatic win in the Breeders Cup Mile at Belmont Park that October when the link between O'Brien and Lester Piggott was reforged. Piggott had already proved that the partnership was a success by riding four winners for O'Brien at the Curragh earlier that month, but Royal Academy's American win was the crowning glory. The horse was then retired to stand at stud in Coolmore, but the profit on his syndication was less than a million, a far cry from O'Brien's earlier massive profits. The failure to produce any other outstanding horses under the Classic Thoroughbreds banner and the depth of the recession in the bloodstock industry gave little hope for the future and the shareholders were faced with a bleak outlook if they were hoping for a return on their investment.

A serious challenger to the O'Brien supremacy was to emerge in the 1980s in the form of Dermot Weld, son of Curragh trainer Charlie Weld. Dermot rode his first winner at the age of fifteen when he steered Ticonderoga to victory in an amateur handicap at the 1962 Galway Festival meeting. In between studying veterinary medicine at University College, Dublin, Weld managed to continue riding as an amateur jockey at home in Ireland, in England, France and America, winning the amateur championship three times. After qualifying as a vet, Weld spent some time working in South Africa before moving to Australia where he took on the post of assistant trainer to T. J. Smyth. He continued his veterinary work out there but, at the beginning of the seventies, his father Charlie decided to retire from training and Dermot returned to take over the reins at Rosewell House. Weld took out a trainer's licence in 1972, ten years after riding his first winner. Thirteen years later, in 1985, Weld was to write another chapter in his biography and Galway was to be the scene yet again when he passed the 1,000 winner mark as a trainer. By the end of that year his tally for the season was 132 victories, which not only netted him just short of £$\frac{1}{2}$ million in prize-money, but brought him agonizingly close to Senator Parkinson's 62-year-old record of 137 winners.

Weld's winnings for the 1989 season went into seven figures following The Caretaker's success in the Cartier Million (made even more poignant by the fact that his mother had bred the filly at her own and Dermot's Pipers Hill Stud) and the two-year-old Go and Go's success in the $300,000 Graded race at Laurel Park in America. Weld still counts Go and Go's win as a particularly important one for Irish racing. The two-year-old was the first Irish- or English-trained horse to win on an American dirt track. The race was originally scheduled to be run on grass, but a deluge resulted in it being moved onto the dirt track. There was no question of withdrawing the colt, however. 'We'd travelled so far for this race that he was running no matter what he ran on. If they'd decided to switch the race onto the main road from Baltimore to Laurel Park he would still have run.'

Weld viewed the victory as a milestone, not just for himself, but for the Irish Thoroughbred industry as a whole. 'We're far too parochial in Ireland, always looking to see what we can beat the British at. Now we've taken on the Americans and beaten them on their own surface, we've proved that the Irish horses don't have to be trained for months to win in America. In the past the Americans have always thought that the American-bred horses adapt to their surface better. We've proved that the Irish horse can do it and that must be a major boost to the sales of Irish-breds.'

Weld's phenomenal success record (he was champion trainer three times during the eighties and also trained the highest number of winners eight years in succession), is a result of sheer dedication and hard work. Up to 100 horses are in training at his two Curragh establishments, Rathbride and Rosewell, and Weld patronizes all the Irish meetings, no matter how small, as well as putting in his bid for the overseas Classics. The first string are out on the Curragh at 8.15 a.m., no matter where Weld has flown back from the night before and, after a quick breakfast punctuated by phone calls from owners, the Turf Club or other racing bodies, it's back out with the second string at 10.15 a.m.

Weld is convinced that much of his success can be attributed to the virtue of playing a waiting game with his equine charges. 'Patience definitely pays dividends. You have to have great confidence in your own ability to be able to wait for the right moment. You have to give horses time to develop and mature if they show potential. If they don't then there's no point in wasting my time or the owner's money. You also have to help educate the owners to have patience. Most are very understanding and don't try to push me into running their horse if I don't think it's ready.'

The individual attention to detail and the man's obvious love for his horses are what count. Weld knows the quirks of each one, what stage its training has reached and when it will be running next, without referring to any files or diaries. Everything is discussed with his number one jockey Michael Kinane, who is down to ride work for Weld each morning,

FAR LEFT: *Schooling over hurdles.*

LEFT: *Former champion apprentice Raymond Carroll and Michael Kinane ready to ride out the first lot from Dermot Weld's Rosewell House yard on the Curragh.*

giving horses their final blow out before a race or assessing the potential of a backward two-year-old before the decision is made whether or not the youngster will be kept in training.

All the horses that are to be run within the next week are worked on the grass gallops in front of the racecourse stands on the Curragh. Everything else is taken onto the all-weather track. Decisions about a horse's future potential are decided only after a work-out on grass. 'Any chance I get I always work on grass. I think it's very important to work horses on the surface they will be running on. If there's any ease in the ground at all I'll work them on the grass rather than the all-weather.'

The two-year-olds that will not be appearing on the racetrack until the following season have been sorted out by the end of October into those that will make the grade and those that won't. The no-hopers go home to their owners, but any that show the spark of a top-class racehorse stay on at Rathbride or Rosewell through the winter.

Michael Kinane, who has been Weld's principal jockey since 1983, explains why. 'It's false economy to send the horses home for the winter. The owners think they're saving money by taking them home, but they lose the condition and muscle that they've built up over the summer and it takes half of the following season to get them back right again. Dermot likes to keep them here through the winter. Horses are like humans, they like to be in familiar surroundings.'

Michael Kinane comes from a winning family. The three brothers, Danny, Tommy and Christy, between them produced nine sons, Michael, Martin, Jayo, Paul, Chris, Tommy jnr., Mick, Paddy and P.P. All twelve have ridden winners under Rules.

Michael's genius is recognized in England as well, and both Henry Cecil and John Dunlop have availed of his services. When Cecil sent Alydaress over to contest the 1989 Irish Oaks at the Curragh, Kinane was given the ride and notched up his first victory in this Irish Classic. Kinane's victory in the 1989 Phoenix Champion Stakes with Carroll House booked him his first ride in the Arc and he lost no time in turning it into a winning debut in Longchamp's biggest race, the day after he had ridden The Caretaker to capture the Cartier Million for Mount Juliet.

But he was straight back to the grindstone the following week and, after a tough work-out with some of the two-year-olds, Weld confers with him about plans for the immediate future and the possible aims for next season. 'There's a lot of pressure put on the two-year-olds,' says Kinane. 'You have to be a bit tough on them, keep working them to see if they've got what it takes. It's no good starting in the spring, it's too late then.'

The Weld formula has undoubtedly proved successful. But of all his winners, one stands out from the rest, the filly Blue Wind, which claimed the English and Irish Oaks in 1981. 'Blue Wind was an extraordinarily talented filly, the best I have ever trained. The day she won the Epsom Oaks she was at her peak and practically unbeatable. Her winning time was two seconds faster than Shergar's Derby. The following week Madam Gay won the French Oaks and she was 12 lengths behind Blue Wind at Epsom. Blue Wind went on to win the Irish Oaks a few weeks later, but she wasn't the same mare. She was at her very best in Epsom.'

Weld also recalls the top-class filly Committed who won the Prix l'Abbaye at Longchamp two years running, Steel Heart, which won the Gimcrack and Middle Park Stakes, and Flash of Steel, the tough miler which won the Irish 2,000 Guineas after a controversial stewards' inquiry. 'I'm the only Irish trainer that won the Irish 1,000 Guineas in the eighties,' he claims. 'Prince's Polly won in 1982 and Trusted Partner in 1988. All the rest were won by either France or England.'

For relaxation Dermot Weld indulges in a spot of National Hunt training as well. 'It's a total hobby for me and the staff rather than having the whole thing go dead from the end of the season until the following April.' But the sport that Weld dabbles in 'purely for fun' brought him the Irish Grand National in 1988 when Brendan Sheridan partnered Perris Valley to win the big race at Fairyhouse. And, although he only has, on average, six jumpers in the yard, Weld retains Sheridan, Anthony Powell and Raymond Carroll to ride for

him and believes that they are invaluable when helping with the sharper young horses that are being aimed for the flat.

The pressure of training such valuable bloodstock is not something that affects Weld. 'There's no point letting the pressure get to you. You have to have a lot of confidence in your ability. You are constantly making decisions, so you get plenty of practice. I just enjoy the job.'

Although Weld believes that the influx of Arab money into the racing and breeding industry in Ireland during the eighties was a good thing, preventing the constant export of the best Irish bloodlines to America, he is aware of the fickle racing public's demand for a more immediately tangible favourite.

Paddy Mullins, who was catapulted into the international limelight by the brilliant mare Dawn Run, agrees that the Irish punter needs his local hero and will not go racing to support foreign millionaires. 'The race-going public wants personal involvement. They want to know the owners and trainers and be able to ask them how their horses are running. They want the inside information. Since the prize-money at the top got good enough to attract the foreigners, the thing has gone into reverse. Racing attendance has declined and, in the last few years, tracks have been closing and falling down in disrepair.'

But Mullins certainly managed to produce a national hero in Dawn Run, even though the press did not always take his side in the constant battle with owner Charmian Hill about who would ride the mare. The Irish racing public had taken Dawn Run to their hearts, however, and the ecstatic scenes as she was led into the winner's enclosure after winning the 1986 Gold Cup are still fresh in the memories of the thousands of fans who flocked to Cheltenham and the more numerous hordes who crowded round televisions in the pubs and bookmakers' shops of Ireland. But even before the mare added this jewel to an already glittering career, Paddy Mullins was aware that Dawn Run had been adopted by the Irish public *en masse*. 'We realized that Dawn Run was no longer trained here and that Mrs Hill was only her nominal owner. The general public owned and trained her.'

The story of Dawn Run's career, the fighting spirit that gave her that Gold Cup victory in spite of almost certain defeat over the last and that final fatal run in Auteuil are all told in the following chapter, but Paddy Mullins has earned his place in the record books with other winners. 'Dawn Run was way ahead of the rest, but there were others that did plenty of winning for us.'

From his Goresbridge, Co. Kilkenny yard Mullins has produced four Irish Grand National winners, three Galway Hurdle winners and Charmian Hill's home-bred mare Boro Quarter to win the prestigious Galway Plate. Like all successful trainers, his drawing room is crammed with crystal and silver trophies. 'That's yesterday's haul,' he says, as he points out a mahogany box containing two bottles of brandy

A jockey's day usually starts very early. A glorious summer's morning is reward in itself, but it is not so easy on a wet day when the rain makes man and horse miserable.

and two glasses following a win at Leopardstown. 'The other two glasses got broken last night!' The Golden Spurs award, presented by the English bookmaking firm William Hill, came his way as leading National Hunt trainer in England for the 1985/86 season. Vincent O'Brien is the only other Irish trainer to have been given this accolade.

Mullins officially started training in 1954. Prior to that his father William had held the licence, but Paddy had done most of the training. His earliest riding experiences came with his father's pack of hounds, the Mount Loftus Harriers, and it was not until 1941, at the age of twenty-two, that Paddy had his first ride on a racecourse. 'It was in a hunter chase at Naas. There were thirty runners, they didn't have ballotting in those days. I know that I finished, but I didn't get anywhere near.'

It was not until two years later that he rode his first winner, which he proudly describes as 'a McCalmont reject'. Trained by Paddy under his father's name, Some Chicken had been named by the McCalmonts following Churchill's famous retort to Hitler's threat that he would wring the British neck like a chicken. 'Some chicken, some neck.'

The horse had originally been intended as a hunter for Major Dermot McCalmont's second wife June. But he turned out to be a diabolical jumper and, when several of the hunt servants had been injured in falls with him, the horse was passed on to a neighbour of the Mullins' after which it joined the Goresbridge yard to go into training. As the young Paddy Mullins left the weigh room at the family pack's point-to-point, where Some Chicken was to make his debut, Major

McCalmont called across the field, 'What are you riding, Mullins?' On being told that his mount for the day was Some Chicken, the Major walked over and solemnly shook hands with Mullins with the words, 'Well I'll say goodbye to you then'. The farewells proved unnecessary, however, and Some Chicken duly provided Paddy Mullins with his first entry into the winner's enclosure.

When he took out the trainer's licence in 1954 Paddy and his new wife Maureen moved up the road from the family home to a rented house that they were later to buy. There were no stables, only what son Tony describes as 'two duck houses'. But that Easter Paddy brought out Flash Parade II to win the La Touche Cup at Punchestown. The horse was owned by a Mr Brown of Castledermot, but Paddy trained

Michael Dempsey, Master of the Galway Blazers and a trainer, uses Galway Bay to swim one of his equine charges in the build-up to a race.

Breaking yearlings at Kildangan before the start of their racing career. This is not always an easy task and the youngsters have to be accustomed to all the breaking tackle and saddlery before a rider is put up on their backs.

and rode the winner over the famous course that still consisted solely of banks and a stone wall.

In those days he had only nine or ten horses in training. Now as many as fifty fill the yard and Paddy says he never has enough room. 'The boys are always buying store horses.' But he laughs at the suggestion that these youngsters are backed and broken before being sold on. 'Sold on? Sold in more like. It does make space a problem. It would be nice to have an idle stable about the place. And one of the major snags is that virtually nobody will buy a horse from me. They all say that if I'm selling it it can't be any good!'

Paddy Mullins gave up riding in 1959 following a bad fall in a bumper at Limerick Junction, after which he spent six weeks in hospital with a back injury. Now the yard is a real family affair. Paddy's wife Maureen plays a major role in the day to day organization. Willie, amateur champion in 1985, 1988 and 1989, still rides for his father, while George works in the yard. Daughter Sandra, although married, still finds time to ride winners for the home stable.

Tony, who has been champion National Hunt jockey on several occasions, including the year that Mrs Hill so controversially jocked him off Dawn Run, has started his own yard near Gowran Park racecourse. The rides are now divided between Tony and his wife Margaret since Tony took out his trainer's licence in 1987.

In Charmian Hill's mind Tony Mullins was never the jockey for Dawn Run. She had planned to ride the mare herself having bought her for 5,800 guineas at the Ballsbridge sales in November 1981 as a three-year-old. But, as Paddy Mullins recalls, she had had so many falls, that the authorities refused to renew her licence in 1982. 'I remember her riding in a hurdle race at Clonmel on a horse called Sun Dancer in the early seventies. The horse dumped her and the stipendiary steward came over to me and told me that this woman should be stopped from riding. Her husband, the late Dr Hill, was standing next to me so I told the steward to talk to him. The steward turned to him and said, "Your wife shouldn't be allowed to ride any more" and Dr Hill calmly replied, "Well you stop her".'

Charmian Hill was, in fact, the first lady rider in Ireland or Britain to take on the male jockeys on the flat, finishing third on her first outing in January 1974. Less than a month later Rosemary Rooney, champion lady rider the previous year, became the first woman to win an amateur race in Ireland, while her sister Ann Ferris rode the winner of the 1984 Irish Grand National, Bentom Boy (Rosemary was third on Dawson City) and partnered the Arthur Moore-trained Iriam to claim the Sweeps Hurdle. Sarah Collen scored another first for the ladies when she rode her father's Bold Flyer, trained by Jim Dreaper, to victory in the 1989 Galway Plate.

Sun Dancer was the only horse of Charmian Hill's that did not win in the hands of Paddy Mullins. Yes Man won on the flat, over hurdles and an amateur novice chase, all with Mrs Hill in the saddle. But, when well into her sixties, Mrs Hill broke her neck in a fall from Sun Dancer at Thurles and was to spend months in the rehabilitation centre in Dun Laoghaire. Even this did not stop her, however, and she was back riding within a year.

Dawn Run originally came to the Mullins' yard in March 1982 when Charmian and Dr Hill went away on holiday. But the mare never returned to the Hills' home in Waterford as Mrs Hill's riding days were numbered and a new jockey would have to be found for the four-year-old.

Dawn Run made her racing debut at Clonmel where she finished unplaced with Mrs Hill in the saddle. On her second outing with the mare, this time at Thurles, Mrs Hill, realizing that she had a lot of ground to make up, gave Dawn Run a couple of slaps. In a phenomenal burst of speed the mare scorched through the field to finish fourth. Paddy Mullins takes up the story: 'The mare ran so well and Mrs Hill gave her such an appalling ride that the stipendiary steward warned me afterwards that, if anyone else had been riding her, he would have had them in.'

But it was third time lucky and Mrs Hill's swansong on the racecourse was to be a winning one. Knowing that her licence was not to be renewed, Mrs Hill brought Dawn Run home the winner in a bumper at Tralee, a race that was to launch the mare on her great career and end the race riding days of her owner Charmian Hill.

Even after the tragic loss of Dawn Run four years later, the Mullins/Hill partnership still continued to produce winners, Mrs Hill remaining a faithful client. But Maureen Mullins does not like talking about the mare. She has never watched the video of her Gold Cup win and even the thought of the circumstances surrounding the mare's fatal accident still hurts. Paddy Mullins was obviously affected by the mare's death too, but he still loves to reminisce about the good times when Dawn Run was at her peak. He also enjoys looking back to the less commercial days of his sport, when money was not so plentiful during the Emergency and vividly recalls one of the local riders, Tom Brophy, winning the La Touche Cup at Punchestown in 1944. 'All transport was off the roads during the Emergency, so Tom took the horse, Princess Philippa, on the train from Bagenalstown. They stayed the night with Tom's uncle, who had bred the mare, and then Tom led her beside his bicycle all the way to the racecourse. He'd only ever ridden in point-to-points before that but, on his first ride ever at a racecourse, he won and then took the mare home the same way as he had brought her. He was the real hero of the hour.'

Another hero, whose reign would last for years rather than hours, was Pat (P.P.) Hogan, who crowned himself king of the

point-to-points in the 1930s and 1940s and has never relinquished the title, continuing to train strings of winners from his yard between Bruff and Kilmallock in Co. Limerick. Paddy Mullins can remember seeing P. P. Hogan on his way to a point-to-point near Carlow. 'We were in a pony and trap on our way to the races when I saw Pat Hogan pedalling flat out on a bike. He rode two winners that day, one for Joe Osborne and one for Paddy Sleator. Then he disappeared off into the night on his bike.'

P. P. Hogan was another jockey who claimed the La Touche Cup at Punchestown but, unlike Tom Brophy, P.P. was well used to proving his worth on the racecourse. His La Touche win came in 1942 with the Tom Dreaper-trained Slacker, carrying the crippling burden of 14st. It was P.P.'s third win of the day and he had also notched up a win and a second on the opening day of the meeting.

Quoted as even-money favourite, Slacker was merely putting the icing on a season of point-to-point successes, including the winning of the Joseph O'Reilly memorial cup at the Ward Union Staghounds' fixture in Fairyhouse. A newspaper clipping of the time shows P.P. holding the cup, which is nearly as big as himself. The cup now holds pride of place in the Hogans' kitchen, as P.P. won it outright in 1985 after a terrific tussle with John Magnier. P.P. had trained the winners in 1976 and 1977 but missed out in 1978. He claimed the cup again in 1979 and 1980, but then John Magnier stepped in to win in 1981 and 1982. P.P. finally managed to score the longed for hat-trick with three consecutive wins in 1983, 1984 and 1985 and, when the Staghounds rang looking for the cup back, it was swiftly lodged in the bank until it was agreed that it really was his rightful property and could be replaced amongst the trophies at Rathcannon.

Hogan's career had really started in 1932 when trainer Charlie Rogers had seen him riding two horses that his father, J. P. Hogan, was breaking for Rogers. The two horses were to be tested for their wind but, when the girth broke, the ten-year-old P.P. was legged up onto each in turn and galloped them bareback. Impressed, Charlie Rogers said to J. P. Hogan, 'You'd better give me that boy for the summer' and, as P.P. himself says, he just never came home again.

He rode in his first point-to-point at the age of thirteen, when the courses were still run over banks. 'There were about thirty or thirty-five banks in each race and some of them you could put a car into the dyke they were so big. But you'd be surprised how few falls we got.' In spite of the dimensions of the fences the jockeys had no protection from crash helmets. 'When I started riding we didn't have crash helmets, we just wore a silk cap. I don't remember when I started wearing a helmet. In the hunt members' races you had to ride in your pink coat and top hat.'

Once launched on his point-to-point career, P. P. Hogan became one of the most respected jockeys of the era and, even though increasing weight meant that he never took out a professional licence, as an amateur he had no equal.

His talents were not confined to jump meetings, however, and P.P. looks back on his win in the 1946 Corinthian Maiden Plate with some pride. His mount that day was none other than Cottage Rake, the horse that was to go on to score a hat-trick of victories in the Cheltenham Gold Cup for Vincent O'Brien. Hogan was closely linked with some of the top names in racing, riding for Dorothy Paget and buying-in horses for both Vincent O'Brien and Robert Sangster with enormous success.

But Hogan rarely scored single victories; doubles and trebles were far more common. At a point-to-point in Kilmallock in the forties he had four wins in five races, including winning his own trophy in the open lightweight race. The only reason he did not go right through the card was because he had no ride in the open farmers' race. He rode five winners at both Killarney and Punchestown and it was not just the press who proclaimed him as 'unequalled as a dashing rider either on the flat, chasing or point-to-pointing'.

Not all his wins were straightforward, however. P.P. reminisces about a point-to-point in Lismore back in 1946 when China Cottage fell at the final bank. Hogan managed to hold onto the horse and was given a leg-up by a spectator. But he turned out not to be quite the Good Samaritan he had at first appeared. 'He wouldn't let go of my horse because he had backed the horse behind mine to win. I had to give him three or four slaps with my whip to get him to let go, but I still managed to get up by a short head on the line.'

A delay of a different kind brought about another win for P.P. at one of the Cork point-to-points. On a very misty day Hogan's horse very nearly fell at a bank just before one of three road crossings on the course. 'He was dead beat so I just walked him on down the road. I thought the horses had gone by again but the next minute I heard them coming, so I jumped in behind them and went on and won. I must have missed out about a mile, but it was the only way that horse could have won.'

But P.P. also robbed himself of one apparently clear-cut victory, as was reported in great detail in the newspapers of the time, with blaring headlines stating: 'Won and Lost: A Fair Rider.' The story ran on: 'Mr P. P. Hogan finished first on My Richard in the Open Race at Tara Harriers Point-to-Point

meeting at Dalystown yesterday, but on returning to the unsaddling enclosure he informed Mr T. Dreaper, the trainer of the horse, that he had gone the wrong side of a post. Mr Dreaper immediately directed the attention of the stewards to the mistake and the horse was disqualified. Flying Marcus was awarded the race.'

A rather more serious brush with the authorities occurred in 1944 when, on 29 July (recorded as his personal D-day in a dog-eared scrapbook), Hogan was called before the stewards of the Turf Club following an inquiry into the running of Shangri at Powerstown Park. The result of the inquiry was that Hogan lost his licence for a year and, in the same scrapbook, P.P. records that he was reinstated on 31 July 1945, his own VE-day.

The winners kept on coming, but a fall at Punchestown in the early fifties, when Banogue was hit by a loose horse in the La Touche, put P.P. out of action for some time. He broke his neck in the fall, was in a collar for nearly a year and admits that the injury 'slowed me down a lot'. The switch to training, however, did not mean a slackening in the winners produced from the Hogan yard and, even now, after nearly forty years of training, it is rare for a point-to-point meeting not to include a P.P. Hogan horse in its winner's enclosure. It is usually his son-in-law, Enda Bolger, who is signed up to ride. 'I try to get the best. Everybody's looking for the best and I think that's Bolger,' says P.P. Roger Hurley is called in to deputize if Bolger is unavailable.

Failing eyesight does not seem to have hindered Hogan in his quest for winners and a cornea graft has helped considerably. But P.P. is still able to spot a good horse. Some of his best buys have been for Robert Sangster, including the French and Irish Derby winner Assert, who was bought for a mere £16,000 by the astute Hogan. An enormous framed Hermes silk scarf hangs above the stairs, naming just some of the winners that P.P. has found for Sangster.

Having been told that he would never ride again because of his impaired vision, P.P. was still managing to get in about fifteen days hunting a year at the end of the eighties. But he claims that, in his real riding days, he was nothing out of the ordinary. 'I was a natural good horseman rather than an extraordinary jockey. But they were definitely better horsemen in those days. The amateurs nowadays couldn't ride over a course of banks. They ride far too short. In my time you always sat into your horse, there was no such thing as riding short.'

Ted Walsh, who was champion amateur eleven times during the 1970s and 1980s, believes that the modern jockey is just as good as his predecessors, but that racing has been ruined through the interference of the stewards. 'Racing changed from 1980 onwards. There are too many restrictions now. The stewards have destroyed the game with all their new-fangled words and inquiries into everything. It's a high risk game and there are going to be casualties, but they've managed to take the spark out of it.'

In his twenty years of National Hunt riding Walsh was never out of the saddle for longer than two or three weeks, usually as the result of a broken collar bone, one of the most common injuries for jump jockeys. But he acknowledges that, once a jockey has established himself at the top of the tree, he obviously gets better horses, decreasing the likelihood of a fall. 'Being a champion doesn't mean you're better than the others, it just means you get the best chances. And once you're established at the top, unless you do something drastic, you can stay there.'

Ted Walsh certainly did stay there, claiming the amateur championship six times in succession between 1972 and 1977, a feat which he attributes to the gap at the top following the retirement of several jockeys. 'I was lucky that I was around just when Francis Flood and Billy McLernon were coming to the end.'

Billy McLernon's dominance of that era brought about the restriction on amateurs, allowing them to ride against professionals on only twelve horses not owned by their immediate family. The professional jockeys had complained that Billy Mac was taking too many of their rides. Billy Mac decided that it was too late in his life to turn professional so he gradually eased himself out of the game. 'There was a lull and racing was waiting for someone to step into their boots. I was old enough to have sense but young enough to have a go,' stated Walsh.

He had his first ride at the age of sixteen, in a bumper at Leopardstown in 1966. But it was in the following year that he scored his first win, dead-heating with Dessie McDonough at the Ward Union point-to-point. Ted's winning mount was Felspar, a horse which he had been given as a present by the owner through Toss Taaffe.

Walsh rode his first winner on the racecourse in 1969. Riding for Toss Taaffe again, Ted steered Buachaill Brega first past the post in a hunter chase at Limerick on St Patrick's Day, 17 March. The following year Ted rode twelve winners, but his career really took off in 1971, while riding for Peter McCreary. From then on he was virtually unbeatable, finally hanging up his boots after winning the Foxhunter Challenge Cup at Cheltenham in March 1976 with the Mouse Morris-trained Attitude Adjuster. 'I'd no idea beforehand. I just decided as I came back in that now was the moment to retire.'

During his twenty-year career Ted Walsh rode nearly 550 winners, an all-time record for an amateur jockey. Riding for Pat Hogan, amongst many others, Walsh broke P.P.'s tally of thirty-seven winners in a year with forty-two victories, and then proceeded to smash that with a new post-war record of forty-eight. (Senator Parkinson's son Billy set the amateur record, which remains unbroken, of seventy-two wins in 1915.)

Walsh looks back on Daring Run and Hilly Way as his best horses. But he has also been associated with a lot of good animals on their way up, such as Brown Lad, who won a bumper for him before going on to claim three Irish Grand Nationals, Ten Up, the horse Jim Dreaper trained to win the 1976 Cheltenham Gold Cup, Monksfield and Galmoy. 'I rode fourteen winners in a month one April,' he recalls. 'Three at Clonmel, three doubles at Fairyhouse, Punchestown and in the north and three individual wins as well. I'd be glad to ride fourteen winners in a year now.'

Following the death of his father Ruby early in 1991, Ted took over the licence and now trains a small string of between twelve and fifteen horses at Kill in Co. Kildare. Since 1983 he has been a regular commentator with RTE, the Irish television network. It is a job he enjoys and he keeps the Irish racing public amused and informed with his down-to-earth comments. His tipster column for *The Star* also brings in a regular cheque, a luxury he says he is getting well used to. He still rides in bumpers, but admits that he misses the thrill of the National Hunt circuit. 'But that's one chapter I can't go back to. I've no regrets about those years. I had very few downs and loads of ups. I couldn't have asked for anything better.'

Another who was dealt a good hand by fate is Jim Bolger who, in 1990, finally eclipsed Senator Parkinson's record which had stood since 1923. Bolger recorded 125 winners on the flat (beating Dermot Weld's 1985 flat record of 120) and a

The all-weather gallops on the Curragh are used by hundreds of horses each day, although many trainers will only work their horses on grass in the final countdown to a race to acclimatize them to the surface they will be running on.

further 22 over the jumps, smashing Senator Parkinson's 68-year-old record of 137 winners overall, but still missing out on the champion trainer award which went to Dermot Weld for the fourth time. Weld, who produced the greatest number of winners on fourteen occasions in his first nineteen years of training, was forty-three short of Bolger's flat tally in 1990, but topped the trainers' earnings table after Rinka Das' victory in the final Cartier Million. Included in Bolger's record-breaking total was Nazoo, unbeaten in her four starts as a two-year-old. Maktoum Al Maktoum's filly wound up her 1990 season by taking the Tattersalls Tiffany race at Doncaster. The officially recorded prize-money awarded to the winning owner was just over £21,000, but Bolger's skills with the filly netted a cool £½ million bonus for the Doncaster victory. However, Jim Bolger's record was broken only a year later. Dermot Weld's tally for 1991 was an outstanding 149 winners.

Although Jim Bolger was born into a horse-coping family in Co. Wexford, he forsook the immediate lures of the equestrian world and moved to Dublin where he became involved in an even speedier type of horse power, as accountant to a large car dealer. His links with racing

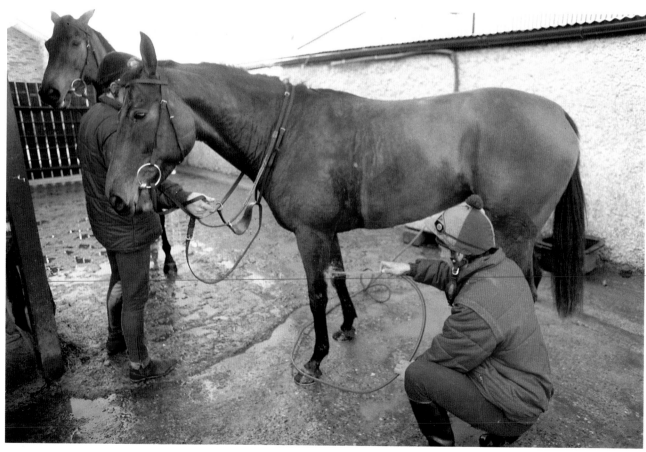

RIGHT: Hosing the horses down after work provides an ideal opportunity for checking the tendons for knocks or strains which could cause problems if left untreated.

continued, however, on a purely social level, but a series of successful betting coups prompted Bolger to take a different sort of gamble and he sank his capital in a tiny yard at Clonsilla, just outside the Phoenix Park. He took out a permit and trained his small string in the Park itself. Included in that string was My Hollow (by Wolver Hollow), owned by Lady Nugent. The filly, who resided in the hen house at the Clonsilla yard, went on to be a Group winner and set Bolger on the path to future glory.

With a few winners already under his belt Bolger took over the stables at Lohunda, just up the road from his own yard, following the retirement of Sir Hugh Nugent. More successes came his way and, by the early eighties, Bolger had raised sufficient funds to buy new premises – the Co. Carlow summer residence of a Church of Ireland bishop in the hills just outside Leighlinbridge. The undulations of the surrounding countryside were to prove a boon to Bolger and the steep all-weather tracks on his new gallops were ideal for testing and improving the stamina of his horses. He seems to have particular success with fillies, and names such as the champion two-year-old Park Appeal and Park Express, both by Ahonoora, as well as the 1991 English Oaks winner Jet Ski

Jim Bolger with, in the background, Dr Michael Smurfit's Chirkpar.

Lady (ridden by stable jockey Christy Roche, who had equalled Michael Kinane's record of 113 winners to take the jockeys' championship the previous year) have all enhanced Bolger's reputation. Five winners in one remarkable day at Gowran Park in August 1991 showed that Jim Bolger has come a long way since his humble beginnings in Clonsilla.

CHAPTER SIX

NATIONAL HUNT AND POINT-TO-POINT

WHATEVER ELSE the horse people of Ireland lay claim to, and they will take credit for virtually all things equestrian if given the opportunity, there can be no disputing the fact that Ireland really is the home of steeplechasing.

This unique form of racing was first recorded in 1752 when two gentlemen, a Mr Edmund Blake and a Mr O'Callaghan, challenged each other to a cross-country race between Buttevant church and the St Leger church in Doneraile, Co. Cork, a distance of $4\frac{1}{2}$ miles. The course was over completely natural country and the two opponents had only the distant church steeple in Doneraile to guide them. But this was the birth of steeplechasing and, although the sport has grown

beyond recognition since then, races very reminiscent of the original are still held by some hunts in Ireland with horses tackling the type of fences they would meet in a day's hunting, and in Ireland these can be imposing to say the very least.

P. P. Hogan, who was king of the point-to-point world as a jockey and still remains on his throne as a trainer, took part in a revival of the original steeplechase in 1954, just over 200 years after that very first race.

The twentieth century version was run in reverse, from Doneraile to Buttevant, but there were rather more runners on this occasion. Seven hunts sent teams of three and, in total, there were nearly seventy starters. Needless to say not

---

OPPOSITE: *Action from the North Tipperary point-to-point.*   ABOVE: *The bookies keep an eye on the race.*

everybody finished and, in one massive pile-up, film director John Huston was one of the many jockeys that hit the deck. But proving that he was still the force to be reckoned with, P. P. Hogan crossed the line first on his own horse Bay Park II. The trophy, a hefty beaten copper shield depicting runners and riders in the 1752 chase, sits at the top of the stairs in the Hogan household.

But how many other countries can also claim the all-time greats of steeplechasing: Arkle, Golden Miller, Red Rum, the brilliant mare Dawn Run who was lost to racing before she had realized half her potential? The list is endless, but Ireland undoubtedly has a knack of breeding and producing the type of chaser that can take on and beat the best in the world.

For many years Aintree and Cheltenham were completely dominated by the Irish-bred horse. That may not be quite so true now with the advent of more scientific breeding techniques which have resulted in other breeds challenging the supremacy of the Irish horse but, on his day, the Irish-bred seems to have the ability to outjump and outstay all his rivals and, in doing so, capture the hearts of the racing public and, in some cases, even the cynical minds of the press corps. These horses become household names, even amongst people who normally have scant interest in the racing scene. But it takes something special, a particularly rare quality, to play on the emotions of the hardened racing journalist.

In their time countless Irish horses have done just that, but perhaps none more so than the legendary Arkle. The British daily *The Guardian* summed up the feelings of more than one nation when it proclaimed in a 1965 editorial that Arkle was 'undoubtedly the fastest 3-miler in the history of racing,' declaring that only Golden Miller (also Irish-bred) could compete with him for the accolade of the greatest chaser of all time. Derek Malcolm, whose eulogy on the great horse appeared in the issue dated 28 December, expressed his concern for the ability of the racing press to continue writing about Arkle in a rational fashion. 'The capacity of sporting journalists to wax lyrical in face of the exceptional is only matched by the speed with which they run out of adjectives in doing so. In the case of an outwardly placid bay gelding called Arkle, the point of no return was reached long ago.'

Bred by the Baker family in north Co. Dublin, the 1957 son of Archive was adored by all. Whoever it was that scrawled 'Arkle for President' on a Dublin wall probably was not joking. Even the official handicapper paid his own tribute to the great horse when, in September 1964, he created two separate handicaps for races, a handicap with Arkle and a handicap without him.

The punters truly loved this great horse who was bought for 1,150 guineas by Anne, Duchess of Westminster as a three-year-old at the Ballsbridge sales in August 1960. Having won twice in his first season of just six races, Arkle went on to win an incredible twenty-seven of thirty-five starts, including the Irish Grand National, three Leopardstown steeplechases, three Cheltenham Gold Cups and two Hennessy Gold Cups. In doing so he virtually eclipsed the career of Mill House, the Co. Kildare-bred winner of the 1963 Gold Cup at Cheltenham whose claim to superstar status simply could not withstand the challenge issued by his rival. Nearly always burdened with the top weight and, on occasion, giving as much as 3 stone to his rivals, Arkle was only once unplaced, crowning his succession of victories with that brilliant hat-trick in the Cheltenham Gold Cup between 1964 and 1966 with Pat Taaffe in the saddle.

Even Taaffe's fellow jockeys were forced to admit, if somewhat grudgingly in a few cases, that they were witnessing a super hero. But some of their comments are worth recording. 'The b . . . went past me as if I were a double-decker bus. He'd have won with the whole Taaffe family on his back,' said one of Taaffe's contemporaries, having been left standing by Arkle's incredible turn of foot. 'There wasn't anything I could do,' another jockey was heard to say. 'I'll swear he was laughing as he passed.'

But the wonder horse was to prove his vulnerability, not to the challenge of others keen to push him from the vaulted position he occupied, but to injury. Tragically the cracked bone that forced his retirement also, ultimately, ended his life. Arkle fractured a pedal bone (part of the skeletal structure within the hoof) at Kempton Park on 27 December, 1966 at the second fence. He gamely battled on to finish runner-up to Dormant, but his racing career was over and, in spite of the best veterinary medicine, nothing could be done to save this brilliant example of Irish breeding.

His skeleton holds pride of place in the Irish National Stud at Tully on the outskirts of Kildare town showing, all too obviously, the injury that removed this equine hero from his adoring public. As Derek Malcolm so rightly said, all the eulogies had been used up and the horse, bereft of the necessary equipment, could not even be retired to stud where he could perhaps have sired progeny which would emulate his remarkable track record. 'If he was an entire, in the racing world's delicate parlance, he would certainly have multiplied exceedingly during his retirement, and at enormous expense. But alas, he is not — and whoever was responsible must be kicking himself from here to Tipperary. There'll only be one Arkle. Perhaps, for the sake of one's adjectives, it's just as well.'

But Arkle was on the stage when steeplechasing had become an established sport, run under rules which, hopefully, produced the fairest result possible. But in those early chasing days of the mid-eighteenth century, when even flags were a luxury, rules were virtually non-existent or were made up on the spot to suit the occasion.

In the days before jump races had become part of the official calendar, competitions restricted to hunters were held on the flat. The qualifications were similar to those now used for point-to-pointing, although in those days the wording was rather more specific, stating that the races were open to hunters 'that have been at the death of a brace of foxes or a leash of hares last season'. But it was some time before obstacles were introduced at the race meetings themselves, and even when they were they weren't included in the actual races, merely being used as another method of qualification.

In 1775 hunters entered for the races at Londonderry on 9 August, which were to be run off in three 4-mile heats, were required to, 'between the hours of nine in the morning and four in the afternoon, leap back and forward over a wall, made from stone and lime, 4ft 2in high and 9in broad at the top, and

day counterparts and there are numerous tales of the proverbial wool being pulled over their eyes. One example saw the stewards awarding a race to a horse which had not only been given a lead over one of the fences, but had actually jumped after the wall had been partially demolished by a so-called 'indifferent spectator'.

It was to be another fifty years before a ruling was brought in to disqualify a horse which had been given a lead by someone not in the race and, until then, infringements of the unwritten rule were all too common as mounted spectators offered assistance or hindrance, depending on who was winning. But the mayhem was not always caused by outside influences. In a steeplechase held at Lismore in January 1819, the winner is recorded as having had four falls, the third-placed horse six and two others one apiece.

The Galway festival meeting has always attracted massive crowds and, particularly on Galway Plate day, all eyes are on the horses.

also over a drain 10ft wide, carrying 12st before judges that were appointed.'

Fifteen years later the fences were to be included in the actual races and, for the first time, handicaps were brought in to take into account both age and previous form. Also in 1790 the first references to the Turf Club are to be found, some thirty-eight years after the English Jockey Club came into being. As yet the term steeplechasing had not been used. The sport was referred to as 'steeple-hunting' or 'steeple-racing' in England, but it was not until 1807 that the Irish Racing Calendar referred to a 6-mile 'steeple-chase' that had been run the previous year.

The new Turf Club had plenty of opportunity to flex its muscles and disputes were constantly being referred to it. So much so that in 1810 the stewards demanded that objections could only be lodged on the payment of one guinea. But the stewards unfortunately were not as astute as their modern-

Although flat racing was beginning to take on some order through the addition of new rules and regulations by the Turf Club, steeplechasing was still very much a sport run by the participants for the participants. Individuals were constantly challenging each other and these matches would often degenerate into the cross-country equivalent of a puissance competition, speed having little to do with the result.

The sport in Ireland was continuing to progress, but the emphasis had now shifted to the west and the meeting at Kiltulla in Galway, which was held annually from 1821 to 1867, usually included a steeplechase on the card. In the 1830s the spring meeting in Mayo featured a 4-mile chase which was run on each of the three days. The obstacles however were reduced each day, with the six walls starting at 5ft on the first day, 4ft 6in on the second and 4ft on the last, although whether this was due to inaccurate jumping on the part of the contestants or not is unrecorded.

ABOVE: *Cardsharps are one of the numerous attractions at the Galway festival meeting at Ballybrit.*

In 1833 an all-grass 3-mile course was laid out at Cahir in Co. Tipperary for the New Melton Stakes. The course included thirty-two fences and, like most chases of that era, simply involved going out and back, with a flag at the furthermost point and the finish through a roped-off chute. The enthusiasm of the crowd, however, even without the benefit of betting which few could afford, caused its own problems, as recorded by Harry S. Sargent, a rider and writer of some note. 'As soon as the leading horse passed everyone closed in, unmindful of those behind, which had either to charge the crowd or be pulled up. I saw many a man ridden over, nearly all were hurt, while some were killed outright.'

Hideous collisions between the racing horses and those of the mounted stewards, who were attempting to keep order, were also frequent. But if the mounted stewards failed to accompany the combatants out into the country, all kinds of dubious practices would break out with rival jockeys being dragged from their saddles or horses being deliberately baulked by other riders or by spectators enlisted for the purpose.

In England the situation was somewhat different. The wealthier climate had allowed the sport to grow into a business and it was a natural progression when Aintree staged its first steeplechase on an enclosed course in February 1836 in response to the demand for more defined tracks and better viewing. The Grand National was launched upon the British racing and betting public three years later, but the unnatural fences did not meet with the approval of the Irish, who felt that such obstacles destroyed the element of danger in steeplechasing which was one of its magic ingredients.

However, northern Ireland trainer Tom Ferguson had three horses entered for the race and it was Ferguson who brought about the naming of Bechers Brook. Approaching the fence on the second circuit Ferguson decided that something had to be done about Captain Becher and Conrad, who were progressing rather too well for his liking. The horses rose upsides over the fence, but on the landing side Becher was floundering in the brook while Ferguson and his horse Daxon galloped on alone. The Irishman got his comeuppance shortly afterwards as Daxon fell while Ferguson's much-fancied runner Rust was kept hemmed in by the other jockeys. Manoeuvred off the course, Rust was officially listed as 'pulled up'.

Twelve months later another of the famous Aintree fences was christened, again with an Irish flavour. John Power of Clonmel had laid a substantial sum of money on himself to be first over the stone wall, which had been included specifically in response to the Irish lobby the previous year. Power and his horse Valentine sped off at a breakneck pace and were first at the wall to win the bet, while ten other horses fell there, including the previous year's winner Lottery. But the reckless pace told in the end and Valentine virtually ground to a halt at the following brook, screwing over it and only surviving by a miracle, after which the fence was renamed Valentine's Brook.

In 1847 Ireland recorded her first victory in the Aintree Grand National when John Courtney's Mathew, ridden by Denny Wynne, won by a length from another Irish-bred, St Leger, in a time of 10 minutes 39 seconds. Another Irish horse, the thirteen-year-old mare Brunette, was also in the reckoning, finishing sixth. The mare was probably not at her best as she had been a doubtful starter due to a cold, but she had beaten both Mathew and St Leger in the Kilrue Cup at Ashbourne the previous year. Brunette had virtually made the Kilrue Cup her own having won the inaugural race at the Co. Meath Grand National Steeple Chase in 1843 and remained unbeaten in the three following years. St Leger also wrote his name into the record books later that year as the first Irish-bred to win the Grand Steeplechase de Paris and claim the then incredible sum of £990 in winnings. These were the famine years in Ireland and the performances of Irish horses both at home and abroad were the one bright spot in an otherwise desperate period in Irish history.

The new decade was to bring more Irish success on the turf at Aintree when the diminutive Abd-el-Kader, known to his connections as Little Ab, became the first horse to win the Grand National on two successive occasions. His victory in 1850 was one of many Irish whitewashes as the first four horses past the post were all Irish-bred. Little Ab came back to Aintree in 1851 to win again, a feat that was not to be repeated for eighty-five years when another Irish-bred, Reynoldstown, romped home the winner in both 1935 and 1936. And the Irish horse staked its claim to another place in the record books when Wanderer, winner at Aintree in 1855, became the first stallion to win the Grand National. His victory was not widely acclaimed, however, as Wanderer, described in the press as 'a rough, under-sized, common-looking hunter', had been entered as a pacemaker for the other Irish horse, Boundaway, who failed to stay the distance.

Back in Ireland the now famous course at Punchestown, which stages Ireland's equivalent of the National Hunt festival at Cheltenham, appeared in the Irish Racing Calendar. Although racing had been going on at Punchestown since the mid-1840s, it was in 1850 that it featured in the calendar as the venue for the Kildare Foxhounds annual meeting at the beginning of April. Four years later Punchestown staged its first two-day meeting although the fences, unlike the ones at Aintree, were still in their natural state. The man behind the rise to fame of the Co. Kildare track was the Marquis of Drogheda, who had taken over where the early benefactor of Irish racing, Lord Waterford, had left off.

In 1861 a seven-race card was published for the Kildare and National Hunt Steeple Chases at Punchestown with a prize

The infamous Punchestown double bank, which is still used in the La Touche Cup at the festival meeting in April and at the three-day event in May. Traditionally steeplechases and point-to-points were always held over bank courses, although not all fences were of such massive dimensions as the Punchestown double. But in 1960 bush fences were introduced at Punchestown and, a year later, the first hurdle race was held there.

fund of £770. The Kildare Hunt Cup was open to members only, but the 3½-mile National Hunt Steeple Chase was open to all and attracted a field of twenty-seven. The following year the feature chase was run over the course now used for the Conyngham Cup, including the famous double bank which still causes spectacular spills even to this day. But it was not until 1865, three years later, that the Marquis Conyngham presented his cup and a purse of 300 sovereigns.

Punchestown played host to the Prince of Wales in April 1868 and huge crowds descended on the Co. Kildare racecourse, determined to catch sight of the future King of England. It is estimated that as many as 150,000 flocked to Punchestown on the first day of the meeting, but on the less crowded second day the Prince was able to ride around the course and see for himself the awesome dimensions of the Punchestown double.

With or without the draw of royalty, however, Punchestown is one of the most popular meetings in the calendar and the three-day National Hunt festival in April always draws enormous numbers of spectators, many of whom head straight across the course to the double bank used in the La Touche Cup. Those who have come just to be seen, however, prefer to do their racing without the assistance of the elements and can be viewed, to their best advantage, draped fetchingly over the chairs in the bar. The hardier ones do brave the fresh air occasionally, just making it to the wild expanses of the grandstand before returning for the next round.

Punchestown was used as one of the qualifying requirements for the new Western Plate at Knockbarron, near Loughrea in Co. Galway in the 1860s. This forerunner of the Galway Plate was worth £200 when it was first held in 1864 and was open to 'gentlemen riders qualified for the National Hunt Races at Punchestown or members of the Co. Galway Hunt'.

Five years later the course at Ballybrit, which now stages

the six-day Galway festival meeting at the end of July, was opened. Thomas Waters, who had already designed the courses at Punchestown, Tramore and Cork Park, drew up and executed the plans for the stands and layout of the course. The directors of the Midland and Great Western Railway agreed to convey all horses to and from the racecourse free, provided they ran in a race. The Plate was run over a $2\frac{1}{2}$-mile course which included eight fences, two being stone walls.

Fairyhouse joined the growing list of Irish racecourses at the beginning of the 1850s and the Ward Union Staghounds moved their hunt races from Ashbourne to the new Co. Meath course where the British fashion of man-made fences had still failed to make an impression.

In the racing world of the 1860s the true gentleman rider was a rare individual. It was customary for them to pay the professional jockeys to stand down and failure to do so was false economy as Captain Shaw found to his cost, eventually fatally at Youghal in Co. Cork. But tighter rules and regulations were on the way. The Grand National Hunt Steeplechase Committee was set up in England in 1866 and, three years later, the Irish National Hunt Steeplechase Committee was formed by Lord Drogheda who, at the beginning of the sixties, had been nominated as Ranger of the Curragh. As well as being a steward of the Turf Club, Lord Drogheda was to remain a steward of the INHSC until his death in 1892.

The first Irish Grand National was run in April 1870. Run over 3 miles at Fairyhouse, the race was won by a horse called Sir Robert Peel. But the start of what was to become the feature chase in Ireland did not mean the disappearance of Irish runners at Aintree and, the following year, the Co. Limerick-bred gelding The Lamb notched up his second Grand National win at Liverpool, having won there previously in 1868.

And the dominance of the Irish-breds at Aintree continued, with an incredible run of seven successive wins started by The Liberator in 1879. Garrett Moore, son of Curragh trainer John Hubert Moore, is credited on the record books as the owner/rider of The Liberator, although in fact the horse was owned jointly by his father and Plunkett Taaffe. Having been scratched from the 1878 running of the National, The Liberator nearly did not make it to the start the following year either when a dispute arose between the joint-owners, and Taaffe sought an injunction to keep the horse out of the race. The application was refused, however, and The Liberator duly started in Garrett Moore's name. Going on to win at his third attempt over the Liverpool fences, The Liberator provided Moore with the opportunity of becoming only the second owner/rider to win the Grand National.

It was then that Henry Eyre Linde took the stage. Based at Eyrefield Lodge on the Curragh, Linde gave his horses plenty

An aerial view of a packed Ballybrit on Galway Plate Day.

of opportunity to rehearse before the main performance, training them over every type of obstacle they were likely to meet on racecourses both in Ireland and in England. This attention to detail certainly paid off. In 1880 the Linde-trained Empress, named after the Empress Elizabeth of Austria, came home in front at Aintree and, twelve months later, Woodbrook was led into the winner's enclosure by his owner Captain Kirkwood and trainer Henry Linde. Linde notched up another important double in 1882 and 1883 when he won the Grand Steeplechase de Paris at Auteuil, both times with four-year-olds, offering even more convincing evidence that his training methods were little short of brilliant.

It was only in 1884 that the running of qualifying heats in steeplechases was outlawed by the Irish National Hunt Steeplechase Committee. The INHSC had been meticulous in its attention to drawing up the rules for chasing in Ireland, so much so that they numbered nearly 190 in 1889.

Ironically, the successes of the Irish horses on foreign

It's hard work getting the hurdles hammered home before the start, but the horse is no respecter of this and the hurdles come in for a great deal of punishment during a race.

tracks were to cause a slump in popularity for the jump meetings at home. The top horses were being syphoned off to lay claim to the lucrative pickings on offer in England and France and mediocre fields or, even worse, small fields did nothing to encourage the crowds to support official race meetings. Their preference lay in the now all too prevalent flapper meetings, a rash of which had broken out in the west of Ireland, apparently as a reaction against the stringency of the INHSC rulings. These flapper meetings were run outside the INHSC rules and horses that ran at such unauthorized meetings were officially barred from running under rules. But there were always loopholes and owners merely changed their horses' names to prevent identification.

But the public at least had some heroes that they were prepared to support at official race meetings. These were the four Beasley brothers, Tommy, Harry, Johnny and Willie who, between them, managed to capture virtually every major prize on offer.

Tommy, the eldest, who rode for Henry Linde, won the Irish Grand National in 1876 and 1877, the English equivalent on three occasions, the Conyngham Cup at Punchestown three times and the Grand Steeplechase de Paris. But he was equally good on the flat and recorded victories in the Irish Derby in 1887 and 1891. Tommy Beasley had steered the Eyrefield Lodge-trained Empress to victory in the 1880 Grand National at Aintree and he was back to record another Irish win at the end of that decade when he partnered another mare, Frigate, in 1889.

Younger brother Harry had started training by then and, in 1891, he trained and rode Come-Away to win the Grand National at Aintree, having won the Conyngham Cup in both 1888 and 1890. Both Johnny and Willie claimed the Conyngham Cup, Johnny in 1877 (and the Irish Grand National the following year) and Willie in 1891. Harry Beasley's 1891 Aintree win was the second Irish win of the new decade and, although the Shropshire-bred (but Irish-sounding) Father O'Flynn came home in front the following year, the Irish provided the winners of the next eight Nationals at Liverpool.

Tragically Willie Beasley was to be killed in a fall at the Herd's Garden bank in Punchestown the year after his brother Harry had won at Aintree. Willie's mount, All's Well, came down at the bank and Beasley was kicked in the head. He never recovered consciousness and died a fortnight later. Henry Linde survived Willie Beasley by five years, dying in March 1897. But Harry Beasley continued to ride and produce winners on into the new century, capturing six Sefton Steeplechases at Liverpool and six Conyngham Cups. At the age of fifty-eight he fell with St Colomba's, a horse he both owned and trained, during the Kildare Hunt Cup at Punchestown. Undaunted, however, Beasley remounted and got up to win by a head. Even more impressive, he rode home the winner of the Maiden Plate at Punchestown in 1923 at the age of seventy-one. His first winner at the Co. Kildare racecourse had been forty-four years earlier, but his 1923 win was possibly the most popular of his career.

The world of steeplechasing had altered considerably by the turn of the century. Leopardstown was now an established track, in spite of a rather faltering start in August 1888. One of the newspapers published an epitaph to the new racecourse, following hopelessly inadequate facilities both at the course itself and transport to it at the official opening: 'Sacred to the memory of LEOPARDSTOWN, foully and brutally strangled at birth by gross incompetence, bungling and mismanagement.'

The new course survived such attacks, however, and its artificial fences sounded the death knell of the old-style steeplechases. Point-to-pointing, originally known as Red-Coat or Sportsman's Race Meetings, had taken over as the new sport, but its popularity was fairly swiftly stamped upon by the INHS Committee, which was determined not to allow this amateur branch of the sport to interfere with the more readily controllable steeplechasing on enclosed racecourses.

The threat of Home Rule for Ireland was delayed by the outbreak of the First World War, and racing seemed set to continue untroubled by any outside influences. Even the publication of a notice from the Turf Club in January 1915 forbidding the Curragh trainers to gallop their horses over the Army football grounds did not seem too restrictive. Later that year another statement from the Turf Club declared that because of 'the grave effect that the discontinuance of racing would inflict on the horse-breeding industry' there would be no cancellation of race meetings; ninety-five fixtures were held in 1915. But the Easter Rising of the following year, which broke out while the Ward Union Hunt steeplechases were being held at Fairyhouse, meant the start of a period of upheaval throughout Ireland which was to affect more than just the racing world.

Racing did manage to continue throughout the war, in spite of a directive from the British Government that, 'in the national interests' racing in Ireland should be discontinued from 5 May 1917. As a direct result of some impassioned pleading from the Senior Steward, Lord Decies, a slightly modified calendar went ahead, with eighty-one meetings being held.

In 1918, Eamon de Valera, the only surviving leader of the Easter Rising, called a general strike for 23 April, the first day of the National Hunt festival at Punchestown, much to the disgust of *The Irish Field*, which doubtless expressed the opinions of many when it stated that 'it was a pity that so many should have been debarred from participating ... as the result of the suspension of the railway service'. Nevertheless, fifty-six race meetings were held in Ireland during 1918. The signing of the Armistice did not mean the end of civil unrest in Ireland, rather the renewal of the disturbances, which were to continue with increasing ferocity until May 1923.

In January of 1919 *The Irish Field*, deploring the request from the Irish Railway executive that racing should be stopped due to the shortage of coal, further compounded fears by stating that Sinn Fein intended to stop both hunting and racing throughout the country pending the release of its imprisoned brotherhood. The paper's fears were amply justified as hunting, outside the six counties of Ulster, ceased almost completely, and numerous point-to-point and steeple-chase meetings were cancelled.

The shortage of coal was still causing problems but, following the resumption of racing at Baldoyle on St Patrick's Day, a slightly reduced calendar was agreed between the Keeper of the Match Book and the Irish Railway Executive Committee which allowed a further eighty-two meetings to be held that year. Strikes in England applied more pressure and, at the end of September, the cancellation of the remaining fixtures in Ireland was ordered. The following day, however, the ban was eased somewhat by the announcement that meetings were merely postponed until coal became freely available again.

Racing went ahead regardless at Limerick that day and the crowds had already gathered for the second day of the meeting when, shortly before the first race, a telegram from Percy La Touche, Senior Steward of the Turf Club, ordered

ABOVE: The winner, bar a fall at the last. The Kildare and National Hunt Steeplechases have been held at Punchestown since 1861 at the instigation of the Marquis of Drogheda. The Co. Kildare racecourse is also the home of Ireland's oldest international three-day event.

LEFT: Leading in a muddied but definitely unbowed The Committee (Liam Cusack up) after coming off best in a gruelling handicap hurdle on the soft at Punchestown.

Boxed up, rugged up and ready to go home after an outing to the rough and tumble of the point-to-point.

the local stewards to abandon the rest of the meeting. A small riot broke out when, mid-way through the returning of gate money to the already aggrieved crowd, refunds were stopped when it was discovered that people were rejoining the queue having already received their money. But, just over a fortnight later, racing was back on the calendar, with Gowran Park staging a meeting on 16 October. Even the arrival of the hated Black and Tans did little to halt racing, although the odd meeting was cancelled, notably Punchestown for the second year running.

Over in England the Grand National returned to Aintree in 1919, after a sojourn at Gatwick, and Irish horses came home in front yet again in 1920 (Troytown), 1921 (Shaun Spadah), 1922 (Music Hall), 1923 (Sergeant Murphy) and 1924 when the 25/1 Donegal-bred Master Robert won.

The 1921 race was notable for the fact that, of the thirty-five starters, the winner Shaun Spadah was the only one that managed to stay on his feet throughout the race. This feat had been achieved ten years previously by Glenside, bred in Ireland but raced solely in England. Incredibly, the same circumstances arose in 1928 when Tipperary Tim, bred in Co. Tipperary, was the only non-faller and held on at the line to win, as Foinavon was to do in 1967.

Back in Ireland the civil unrest, which had started in earnest in January 1919, finally came to a halt in May 1923. In the interim, the Sinn Fein candidates elected as Members of the British Parliament in the General Election of 1918, had set up a separate Irish parliament, Dail Eireann, with Eamon de Valera as President.

The departure of the British in 1922 and the establishing of the Irish Free State had served to heighten tension rather than reduce it but, on 24 May the following year, Eamon de Valera ordered a cease-fire and the civil war was over. But it was to be a year of strikes and, in February 1924, the stable boys at the Curragh downed tools in a protest against pay cuts. Racing at Leopardstown went ahead, however, unaffected by the stable boys' action.

The rules governing steeplechasing were still being tightened up, both in Ireland and in England. One loophole which continued to cause trouble was the use of substitute riders — in the middle of a race! Under National Hunt rules fallen horses can be, and indeed are, remounted. Many people

If you cannot get any four-legged horsepower, two wheels will do to save your own legs.

will remember Tony Mullins clambering back on board Dawn Run after falling at the Cheltenham January meeting in the mare's build-up to the Gold Cup. But the rules also allow a substitute rider, providing they can do the right weight, to mount and finish a race if the original jockey is hurt in the fall. It is also specified that no penalty will be imposed for carrying overweight in the case of a substitute rider. It was a substitute rider who brought Timothy II home to win a 3-mile chase at Cork Park in 1913. The original jockey, a Mr J. Murphy, was injured in a fall and his brother, T. Murphy, took his place in the saddle to win.

The rules in England were changed in 1931 to prevent the substitution of riders mid-way through a race, but this is officially still permissible under Irish National Hunt rules. In 1960 Mr H. Kerrigan's horse Bridge Echo fell and got away from him in a chase at Ballinrobe. Glenmore Girl was a faller at the same fence and, while her jockey languished on the ground, Mr Kerrigan vaulted into the saddle and set off in hot pursuit of the field. But his enterprise went unrewarded as Glenmore Girl fell again at the last fence.

The breakaway of the Irish Free State from British rule did not mean the disappearance of Irish horses at Aintree, with seven Irish wins between 1920 and 1930. But the Grand National of 1931 had a special significance for Ireland. Not only did the Co. Carlow-bred Grakle win, but this was also the first steeplechase on which the Irish Sweep was held. Founded the previous year by Richard Duggan, in association with Joe McGrath and Captain Spencer Freeman, the Irish Hospital Sweepstakes paid out £354,724 12s 4d on the winning ticket. Unfortunately, the holder of that ticket, an Italian café owner, had sold three-quarters of his share for £10,000 to a bookie before the start of the race.

The winning horse, Grakle, was by Jackdaw, and his progeny were to provide Ireland with more victories. In 1933 Kellsboro Jack (by Jackdaw) won at Aintree, but it was Brown Jack who really established Jackdaw as a top-class sire. Sold as a yearling for £110, Brown Jack was to change hands again the following year when trainer Charlie Rogers, whose ability to spot young talent is recorded in the previous chapter with regard to P. P. Hogan, bought the horse for £275. He failed to produce any winning form on the flat, however, and was subsequently sold to England where he won five hurdle races in quick succession. The following year he took the Champion Hurdle at Cheltenham before being teamed up with Steve Donoghue, when the horse was switched back to the flat, a decision that was more than justified when Brown Jack won six successive runnings of the Queen Alexandra Stakes at Ascot between 1929 and 1934.

It was during this period that the imposition of customs duties on livestock by Britain threatened to cripple the Irish bloodstock industry and sparked off an economic war betwen

Britain and Ireland. Horses were sold for rock-bottom prices and the top horses were all exported before the newly imposed duties had been brought into effect. This had disastrous repercussions within the industry, including a drastic fall off in attendance at race meetings. Navan racecourse, which had only opened in 1921, was particularly badly hit and was forced to close down thirteen years after its first meeting. But the board stubbornly refused to allow the racecourse to die and, having formed a new company, Proudstown Park (Navan) Racecourse Ltd, reopened the track in 1936.

Another Irish-bred superstar had captured the public's attention by then in the form of Golden Miller, one of the all-time greats of steeplechasing history. But The Miller's parentage was unlikely to excite too much interest and certainly belied the brilliance that was to win his owner Dorothy Paget a record five successive Cheltenham Gold Cups. Golden Miller was by the unraced sire Goldcourt, whose 5-guinea stud fee was probably a direct result of his father Goldminer never having set foot on a racecourse either. The only claim to fame on his dam's side was that she, Miller's Pride, had finished second in a £22 chase at Piltown. The Miller was sold at Ballsbridge for 100 guineas as a yearling, before being passed onto top Dublin showman Nat Galway-Greer. The horse was then exported to England having been bought by the trainer Basil Briscoe for £500, after which he joined the string of Dorothy Paget, who was linked with so many top Irish-breds.

Golden Miller started his dominance of the Gold Cup in 1932 and, two years later, he carried 12st 2lb to win at Aintree as well, the only horse to have won both the Gold Cup and the Grand National in the same year. Twelve months earlier The Miller had been given the same burden, despite the fact that he was only six at the time, to finish second to Kellsboro Jack.

When Golden Miller's winning sequence at Cheltenham came to an end, Reynoldstown shifted the Irish emphasis back to Aintree, winning the National there in 1935 and 1936. (This feat of winning the Grand National twice in succession had previously only been achieved by one other horse, the Irish winner Little Ab.) Reynoldstown was bred in north Co. Dublin and, in his 1935 victory, carrying the colours of his Cork owner Major Noel Furlong, he led home just five other horses, all of which had Irish blood in their veins. The same had been true in 1930, Shaun Goilin's year, when there had been only six finishers and all had been bred in Ireland. The link between the Irish winners continued in 1937 when Royal Mail won at Aintree. Royal Mail was by My Prince, sire of Gregalach (the 100/1 winner in 1929), the dual Gold Cup winner of 1929 and 1930, Easter Hero, and Reynoldstown.

Ireland rapidly came up with another prepotent sire to

replace My Prince at the head of the leading National Hunt sires table. This was Cottage, a horse of savage temperament, who was knocked down to the sole bidder, Michael Magnier of Grange Stud, Fermoy, Co. Cork at the Newmarket sales of 1924. Grange Stud was to become part of the vast Coolmore empire fifty years later. Cottage had won only once himself, but he sired the Grand National winners Workman, Sheila's Cottage and Lovely Cottage, Gold Cup winner Brendan's Cottage and Cottage Rake, trained by Vincent O'Brien to win at Cheltenham in 1948, 1949 and 1950.

The 1940 Grand National at Aintree, the last to be run until after the war, was won by yet another Irish horse, the seven-year-old Bogskar. But it was a further year before Ireland began to feel the effects of war, compounded by an outbreak of foot-and-mouth disease which brought about a ban on racing, hunting, horse shows and polo from the end of March onwards. The outbreak was fairly swiftly contained and, although the Irish Grand National and the Conyngham Cup were both lost, all the other Classics were held that year.

The shortage of petrol and coal from 1942 was less easy to deal with, however, and vehicles of all description were pressed into service to transport the keen race-goers to the action. National Hunt trainer Paddy Mullins recalls how, when cars were officially off the road because of the Emergency, there seemed to be an enormous increase of funerals on race days and, although the empty coffin was not actually laid to rest at the racecourse, the entourage of permissible cars would get as close as possible before the 'mourners' abandoned their vehicles and started walking, rather than risk being caught by the ever vigilant Gardai.

But once again the Irish breeders managed to produce a horse that took the punters' minds off the problems at home and abroad. The newcomer was Prince Regent (a 1935 son of My Prince), who was sold as a yearling to millionaire J. V. Rank for 320 guineas at the Ballsbridge sales. Prince Regent was sent to Co. Dublin trainer Tom Dreaper who brought him out as a five-year-old to win a $1\frac{1}{2}$-mile flat race at Naas. In only four runs over fences in 1941 Prince Regent won three, beaten a short head at Leopardstown by Dorothy Paget's Golden Jack who was by Goldcourt, the sire of Golden Miller.

Now burdened with 12st or over, Prince Regent nevertheless won his first three outings with ease and was then asked to carry 12st 7lb for the Irish Grand National. Although giving Golden Jack 12lb, he managed to turn the tables on his old rival and get home a length to the good for jockey Tim Hyde. Prince Regent succumbed to the weights on his last outing that year, however, going down to Prince Blackthorn. But the two met at Baldoyle the following January when Prince Regent was giving 2st 11lb to the four-years-younger Prince Blackthorn. As Prince Blackthorn approached the last in front, it looked as though the 1942 result would be

repeated. But Tim Hyde galvanized the fighting spirit of a true champion to get Prince Regent home by a neck.

After the war Prince Regent, having won his first race in England at Wetherby, was made favourite for the Cheltenham Gold Cup in which he duly obliged by 20 lengths. But hopes of adding the Grand National to his tally were thwarted when he finished third that year, fourth 12 months later carrying 12st 7lb and was run off course by a loose horse in 1948. The decision to retire him was reversed, however, and the old horse came out to win two further races, one of them at Cheltenham, before he was finally pensioned off at the age of fifteen as one of the turf's most popular veterans.

Although Prince Regent failed to win the Aintree Grand National for his connections, there were plenty of other Irish horses waiting in the wings and seven of them proved themselves up to the task between 1946 and 1955. One of these was Jack McDowell's Caughoo, winner of the 1947 National. Downing champagne with the celebrating Irish contingent in the weigh room afterwards was Aubrey Brabazon, who had fallen at Bechers with Luan Casca. To the consternation of his fellow jockeys, A.B.'s slender figure suddenly crashed to the floor. But it was not the drink that had caused this dramatic loss of consciousness. Internal bleeding had finally made its presence felt, some time after the fall, as Brabazon had ridden in a flat race after the National. He was rushed to hospital where broken ribs and a punctured lung were added to the list of injuries.

'Charlie and Gita Weld, Dermot's parents, had picked me up after the fall. Charlie actually gave me a drink from a baby bottle of Powers. But, because I was warm, I didn't realize I had broken ribs. The French horse I rode later in the day pulled so hard that the ribs turned in and punctured my lung. It was the worst fall I ever got. I damn'd near died and was in hospital in Liverpool for five weeks.'

Luckily, for one trainer in particular, Brabazon pulled through and he was to display his superb skill both over fences and on the flat for another thirteen years.

One who used those skills to conjure up winning performances from the horses he himself had nurtured was Vincent O'Brien, who proved himself unbeatable both at home and in England on the National Hunt scene. It was not until 1959, when O'Brien forsook the jump meetings in favour of the flat that the National Hunt world was able to catch its breath and return to some semblance of normality.

Following O'Brien's three-in-a-row at Aintree with Early Mist, Royal Tan and Quare Times, another trio of Irish-breds claimed the honours in 1956, 1957 and 1958. But 1956 will always be remembered as Devon Loch's year, when the Queen Mother's horse, also bred in Ireland, spread-eagled on the flat only yards from the finish, allowing jockey Dick Francis to see certain victory vanish from his grasp in a moment that is engraved on the memories of all who witnessed it.

The departure of Vincent O'Brien for the glittering lure of the flat world made way for the rise of a new Irish star, Paddy Sleator, who made Punchestown virtually his own in 1953 and 1954. Sleator trained at Grangecon, not that far from Punchestown and also comfortably close to the point-to-point then held at Two-Mile-House near Naas. But P. P. Hogan remembers the distance as being quite considerable when he was made to walk it one night after a slight misunderstanding with the trainer.

At that time it was quite common to enter a horse for two races at a point-to-point and, when P.P.'s mount nearly fell and was pulled up in the first, no-one was surprised to see the same horse reappear in the last, this time with Colette Brown in the saddle. The punters, and P.P., assumed that the horse was merely being taken out for a school so, when P.P. turned in the saddle about five from home and saw the horse going well up to the bridle, he manoeuvred his own mount into its path and baulked it as it went to take off. He unfortunately recounted this to Sleator on the return journey to Grangecon in the pony and trap. '"You were very lucky in the last," I said to him, "I looked round and saw your horse running away with the girl so I had to push her into the wing." He stopped the pony and just said, "You bloody fool, I had him backed at 10/1" and threw me out of the trap. I had to walk all the way back to Grangecon in the dark.'

In spite of such reverses Sleator managed to train the winners of the Kildare Hunt Cup, the Punchestown Cup, the Prince of Wales Plate, the Maiden Plate and the Conyngham Cup at the Festival meeting in 1953 and, twelve months later, collected the Kildare Hunt Cup, Prince of Wales Plate and Maiden Plate again and added the La Touche Cup to his haul.

In 1955 he won the Galway Plate with Amber Point, who notched up a double when coming home in front again in 1956, the year in which Sleator, dubbed the 'Grangecon wizard' by the press, trained the winners of thirty-two National Hunt races and twenty-nine races on the flat. The following year Knight Errant won the Plate for Sleator and followed this up twelve months later by becoming the only horse to win both the Plate and Hurdle. In 1959, however, Sleator set up a record when he saddled the winners of eight races at the three-day July meeting in Killarney.

Of those eight Sleator-trained winners, three were ridden by Bobby Beasley, grandson of the famous Harry Beasley. The following year Bobby Beasley partnered Another Flash to win the Champion Hurdle at a Cheltenham meeting completely dominated by the Irish, with fourteen of the eighteen races falling to the Irish invaders. Beasley went on to win that year's Conyngham Cup at Punchestown and the Galway Plate for the second time and, in 1961, rode Nicolaus

The jockeys' job is to go out and ride, preferably to win. It is the job of the valets, even in the makeshift conditions on offer at the point-to-points, to ensure that the jockeys are wearing the right colours for the next race.

Silver to win the Grand National. This was the year in which the Aintree fences were modified to give more slope on the take-off side. Eighteen years later, after annual controversy about injuries to horses and the occasional fatality, Bechers was altered yet again with the brook being narrowed and the ground on the landing side levelled off to prevent horses rolling back into the ditch.

Changes were taking place in Ireland during the sixties as well with banks disappearing from virtually all courses except Punchestown. The bush fences, which had been used for the Irish Grand National at Fairyhouse since 1939, were introduced to Punchestown in 1960 and, four years later, the Conyngham Cup was abandoned until 1969, when it became a bush fence race. The banks are still used for racing, however, although the big double features only in the 4¼-mile La Touche Cup.

Most of the old guard regretted the passing of the banks. 'I definitely liked the banks better,' proclaimed Aubrey Brabazon, in spite of the fact that he was a genius, not only over all types of obstacles, but on the flat as well. 'I suppose I was lucky because most of my rides were for Joe Osborne and he

The more traditional point-to-points are still held on farmland and not on the local racetrack, so the official outlet for the day's race card is usually a jeep or a horse box.

had them beautifully schooled. I rode a mare for him, Alice Baythorn, to win the Maiden Plate at Punchestown in 1944. The next year she won the Prince of Wales Plate on the first day and then came out to win the Conyngham Cup the next. Brilliant she was. But Punchestown was a two-day meeting then. It was never the same when they went to three and four days and when they took the banks away.'

The banks began to vanish from the point-to-point courses as well, and by 1970 they had all gone, except from the occasional hunt race that was run over natural banks. Both the Black and Tans and the Limericks still organize special races over bank courses which attract entries from all over the country.

Many of the old point-to-point venues disappeared at about the same time as the banks became memories, resulting in a dramatic drop in the number of meetings held. The lowest recorded figure was in 1968 when only thirty-eight point-to-points were run. The fixture list has certainly come back to life now and there are close to eighty meetings held between the beginning of January and the end of May every year.

Virtually every budding jump jockey gets some experience in the point-to-point field. Even Iris Kellett, who went on to become the ladies European showjumping champion, had her share of rides in point-to-points. Her father Harry Kellett trained racehorses before he embarked on his career with showjumpers.

The practice of putting youngsters in their early teens up on point-to-pointers is not one that meets with universal approval, however. Ted Walsh believes that the basis for his successful career was not being allowed to ride in point-to-points at too tender an age. 'My Uncle Ted guided me in the right direction. He didn't let me ride in point-to-points at first. He'd ridden in so many himself over the years, he just made sure I was mature enough before I tried it. He didn't wrap me up in cotton wool. He just knew that sixteen or seventeen is old enough for riding in bumpers, but not for getting falls in point-to-points.'

While Arkle was just embarking on his career in the early 1960s, the Irish horses continued to hit the headlines at Aintree, winning in 1962, 1963 and 1966. And the amateur rider Alan Lillingston, who was to be a member of the Irish gold medal-winning team at the European three-day event championships in Luhmuhlen in 1979, rode the one-eyed Winning Fair to victory in the 1963 Champion Hurdle at Cheltenham.

Winning Fair was trained by George Spenser in Thurles, Co. Tipperary. He was ridden in all his work by Willie Slattery and it was Slattery who accompanied him when he went for a blow-out on gallops owned by Willie O'Grady, father of Edward who still trains at Ballynonty. After Winning Fair and one of O'Grady's horses had finished their gallop, O'Grady

asked Spenser whether he was pleased with the way the horse had worked. Spenser replied that he was, especially as he was blind in one eye. To Spenser's amazement O'Grady then revealed that his horse had also lost the sight in one eye, on the opposite side to Winning Fair. When working upsides, both on their blind side, the two horses had probably never even seen each other!

On the home front in 1966 Tom Dreaper notched up his seventh successive win in the Irish Grand National, while across the water, Red Alligator, a half-brother to the 1966 winner at Aintree, Anglo, kept the Irish to the fore by claiming the 1968 National by 20 lengths. Fort Leney won the 1968 Cheltenham Gold Cup with Tom Taaffe in the

saddle, to record a fifth Gold Cup win for Dreaper and a fourth for Taaffe.

Gold Cup honours continued to come back to Ireland. L'Escargot won at Cheltenham in 1970 for trainer Dan Moore and went on to make history by becoming the first horse since Golden Miller to win both the Gold Cup and the Grand National, recording his Aintree success in 1975 when he beat the crowd's beloved Red Rum. L'Escargot was one of the few Irish-trained horses to win a steeplechase in America when Dan Moore produced him to take the Meadow Brook Handicap Chase at Belmont Park in June 1969.

Pat Taaffe, who had partnered Arkle almost exclusively throughout his reign, produced another winner in the form of

Flagfall at the start of a race at the North Tipperary point-to-point. Even in National Hunt racing the jockeys will usually discuss who wants to go on and make the pace at the beginning.

Captain Christy who, as a first season novice, claimed the 1974 Cheltenham Gold Cup. Bobby Beasley, who had fought off the dual terror of alcoholism and increasing weight, made a superb comeback to steer Captain Christy to this impressive victory. When Beasley decided to call it a day for the second time and left Ireland for good, Bobby Coonan, who had ridden the horse into second place in a hurdle at Naas in October two years earlier, was reunited with Captain Christy who added a further five wins to his tally with Coonan in the plate. In a bold bid to pick off the top French chasers, Captain Christy just failed to make the distance in heavy going to come in second in the Grand Steeplechase de Paris of June 1975. At the end of that year, injuries from a bad fall left Coonan sidelined for Christy's last race, and last win, in the 1975 King George VI chase when he was partnered by young Gerry Newman.

An era came to an end in the seventies, however, with the death of Tom Dreaper that same year. But his son Jim, who had ridden his first winner at Naas at the age of fifteen in 1968, proved a more than worthy replacement for his father, training Colebridge to win the Irish Grand National in 1974 and producing Brown Lad to record three victories in 1975, 1976 and 1978 with Tommy Carberry up. Dreaper did not confine his successes to home territory however and, in 1976, made a raid on the Cheltenham Gold Cup which he took with Ten Up. Mick O'Toole then added his name to the list of winning trainers with Davy Lad in 1977.

There was no shortage of top Irish horses during the seventies, including another who attracted his faithful following of worshippers, Red Rum. Bred in Ireland but trained in England, Rummy still adorns the exteriors and interiors of betting shops everywhere after making the Grand National virtually his own with that incredible run of three victories and two seconds between 1973 and 1977.

But, as the seventies came to a close, there was another equine athlete warming up for the track, the mare Dawn Run, who was to write her own chapter in the record books, in spite of a career cut tragically short. Charmian Hill had set herself a limit of 6,000 guineas when she headed for the Ballsbridge sales in November 1981. She thought that would go nowhere near buying the filly she had set her heart on, a three-year-old by the already popular sire Deep Run. But, when the filly was put on the market at 5,500 guineas Mrs Hill immediately put in her bid of 5,800 guineas and, to her surprise, no opposing bids were made. The filly was knocked down to Charmian Hill's first bid and so began a partnership that was to put the Irish right back at the top of the tree.

Dawn Run joined Paddy Mullins' stable in March 1982, winning at Tralee with Mrs Hill in the saddle three months later. Tom Mullins was brought in as replacement jockey and the mare won at both Galway and Tralee before having a

month's lay-off due to the hard ground. Having been well and truly beaten in the 2-mile Leopardstown Novice Handicap, finishing second last of seventeen in what Paddy Mullins described as 'the wrong race for her', Dawn Run ran in her first hurdle race at Naas on 27 November where, with Peter Kavanagh up, she finished fourth to Seskin Bridge.

Teamed up with Tony Mullins, the mare then won her next two outings, at Navan on 20 December and, eight days later, at Leopardstown in the first of many battles with Buck House and Tommy Carmody. Dawn Run, at 12/1, came home $1\frac{1}{2}$ lengths clear of Buck House. The favourite, Castletown House, another inmate of the Mullins stable, trailed in unplaced.

In her first run of 1983, the mare finished a disappointing sixth after Mrs Hill asked Tony Mullins to hold her up. Both Paddy and Maureen Mullins were away on holiday and Tony warned Mrs Hill that the mare would not finish in the first three if she was not allowed to jump off in front. Early in February Tony and Dawn Run won the Forenaughts Hurdle at Punchestown, making all the running. But, in spite of starting favourite, the mare could only finish third at Leopardstown a fortnight later. Tony Mullins was promptly removed from the saddle for the mare's run in the Sun Alliance Novice Hurdle at Cheltenham the following month. Mrs Hill's explanation was that Tony was too inexperienced to ride in such an important race. Ron Barry took the ride and Dawn Run was beaten into second place, although Paddy Mullins still remains convinced that the mare would have got her nose in front if Tony had been riding.

Three weeks later and reunited with Tony Mullins, Dawn Run made all the running in the Novice Handicap Hurdle at Liverpool to win, pulling up, by 10 lengths. After such an easy race Paddy Mullins brought the mare out again the next day for the Sun Temple Hurdle where she ran that year's Champion Hurdle winner Gaye Brief to a length with the third place horse 20 lengths adrift. 'After that she was in the big time,' says Paddy Mullins. 'The public had decided that that was the end of Dawn Run, for that year anyway. But she came out on 26 April to win the BMW Champion Novice Hurdle at Punchestown by 10 lengths with Buck House back in fifth. After that she was put away for the summer.'

A 2-mile flat race at the Curragh was selected as the mare's autumn debut on 22 October. She finished fourth but won next time out at Downroyal in a condition hurdle on 5 November. With Tony Mullins aboard she won with a 10-length advantage. That evening, Mrs Hill informed Paddy Mullins that she wanted a change of jockey, 'because the mare had drifted to the left slightly at the last'. 'She did allow me to choose who would ride her, even though she was putting down Tony,' says Paddy Mullins. Mrs Hill had specified that she only wanted an Irish jockey so the ride was offered to

When there is no grandstand at the local point-to-point any bit of shelter from the elements will do.

Jonjo O'Neill for a 2½-mile condition hurdle at Ascot in the middle of November. In a controversial photo-finish, Dawn Run beat Amarach by a short head. 'The Hill family immediately said wasn't it a good job Jonjo was on board because Tony would never have got her home in front!'

Back in Ireland the mare was beaten 3 lengths by Boreen Deas, a moderate horse according to Paddy, again ridden by Jonjo. But the pair were back in winning form at Kempton after Christmas, beating Gaye Brief a neck in a terrific finish. 'That was the end of Gaye Brief as a contender for the Champion Hurdle. It was his ground at Kempton, but he was starting to show the white feather.' Gaye Brief was still being quoted as favourite for the Champion Hurdle, however, but the horse was withdrawn a couple of weeks beforehand and Dawn Run was immediately promoted to odds-on favourite.

Of her six runs in 1984 Dawn Run won all six, opening the season with the Wessl Cable Champion Hurdle at Leopardstown on 18 February with Jonjo O'Neill in the saddle. O'Neill steered the mare to victory in the Champion Hurdle at Cheltenham three weeks later but, in what Paddy describes as one of her worst runs, she beat Sima by just half a length.

Shortly before the Aintree meeting Jonjo O'Neill had a fall and was not passed fit to ride the mare in the Sandeman Hurdle, a race in which Dawn Run had finished second to Gaye Brief twelve months earlier. Tony Mullins was reinstated in the saddle and the mare won, pulling up by 10 lengths. 'We were all on a high after that,' Paddy Mullins says. 'I said that we should go for the French Champion Hurdle. No British- or Irish-trained horse had won it before, or since.' The mare fully justified her trainer's confidence and, with Tony Mullins in the saddle, she won her warm-up race in the Prix de la Barka and, less than a month later, won the coveted French Champion Hurdle by 6 lengths to become the first horse to win the feature Irish, English and French hurdle races.

Dawn Run's brilliance over hurdles could have made her one of the biggest money earners of all time. But, from the time she had schooled her as a four-year-old, Mrs Hill had earmarked the mare for the Cheltenham Gold Cup, so Dawn Run was switched to chasing. Tony Mullins was not opposed for the mare's first outing on a chase course and, in front of a record crowd, Dawn Run came home well clear at Navan on 1 November. But a tendon injury did not respond to treatment and Dawn Run was laid off for a year to recuperate.

At the back end of the 1985 season Dawn Run reappeared on the racecourse to score two wins from two runs. Flicking through the form book to remind himself of the details, Paddy Mullins notes that son Tony was still on board, 'but I've an idea he's not going to be on her much longer,' he says with a half-grin.

In the build-up to the Gold Cup, Mullins decided that the mare would have to have a run over the Cheltenham fences beforehand if she was to stand a chance in the big race itself. 'I brought two horses over at the end of January. Tony rode both and got two falls.' Unshipped by an appalling mistake from Dawn Run, Tony nevertheless remounted and went on to finish fourth. 'That,' says Paddy Mullins, 'I've no hesitation in saying, was the winning of the Gold Cup. But it was also the end of Tony riding her.' Returning after a week's holiday, Paddy Mullins was met with a pile of English newspapers, all featuring the Dawn Run story. 'One of them even said, Mullins has gone to Portugal, but he'll have to come back to face Mrs Hill!'

Dawn Run's next outing was the Gold Cup at Cheltenham where the mare showed her true courage by coming back from certain defeat at the last to overtake Wayward Lad and win by a length at the line. But, in spite of acknowledging that it was this performance that 'made her into an absolutely great mare', Paddy Mullins admits that he watched the race without any emotion. 'After the way we'd been treated it didn't mean a thing to me, I watched it without any feeling of any kind and I wouldn't talk to the press afterwards.'

The rest of Ireland celebrated in real style, however. The

The winner's enclosure is always the jockey's goal, no matter where the race meeting.

Winner

Irish versus English battle at Cheltenham is a feature of the festival, but the scenes after Dawn Run's victory are still spoken of, as first Mrs Hill and then Jonjo O'Neill were carried shoulder high by the near hysterical crowd. Jonjo was quick to bring the deposed Tony Mullins back into the picture however, putting him up on his shoulders to get his share of the acclamation.

But both Jonjo and the mare were brought down to earth pretty rapidly with a heavy fall at the first in Liverpool at the beginning of April. 'It's not surprising that a brilliant hurdler would do that,' explains Paddy Mullins.

Back home again, Dawn Run paired up with Tony Mullins to win the much publicized match against Buck House at Punchestown. Mouse Morris, trainer of Buck House, was given the option on the distance and chose 2 miles to suit his own horse. But his tactics did not work and Dawn Run was $2\frac{1}{2}$ lengths clear at the finish.

The final chapter was about to be written, however. Paddy Mullins takes up the story. 'At the behest of Mrs Hill and Oliver we went to France for the Champion Hurdle again. Nobody else wanted to go. With Tony riding she was beaten 3 lengths in the Prix la Barka, which she'd won two years previously, and straight away Mrs Hill wouldn't have Tony for the next run. She did give me the choice of jockey though

and, knowing that the French hurdles are very tricky and the course is in a figure of eight, I wanted a French jockey. Desmond Stoneham got me Michel Chirol. As everybody knows the mare fell. She broke her neck and was killed instantly, that was the one good thing about it. I had opposed it all the time, but was given to understand that if I didn't take her to France, somebody else would.'

On a scorchingly hot day Dawn Run's body was removed from the track immediately. 'Mrs Hill did get to see her, but we didn't get a chance to get a hoof, or a piece of hair or anything.' It was an ignominious end to steeplechasing's greatest mare, who would have undoubtedly gone on to win more races, establish new records and, eventually, produce foals that would follow in her footsteps.

Mrs Hill's famous red coat, which she always wore for luck with a black leather belt to match her racing colours, had been shed in the heat at Auteuil. She never wore it again, giving it away to a charity auction where it was bought by the sole bidder, freelance racing journalist Claire Barry for £40. Mrs Hill was laid to rest in January 1990 and her coat now resides in the museum at Leopardstown in memory of Ireland's favourite equine heroine.

But the pedestal is never vacant for long. Ireland will always manage to produce another superstar, a horse that can capture the imagination and the hearts of the public. The magic ingredients are merely waiting to be combined. And the Irish will continue to flock to Cheltenham in their thousands to join battle with the English yet again. They are prepared to face their first big gamble even before they leave Ireland but, if they get past the currency check without having their contraband sterling officially lifted from their pockets, the folding stuff will disappear all too quickly across the water. There have been some lean years. But the rivalry still remains and the Irish will always be there to take the English on at their National Hunt mecca or at Aintree. And somewhere, at one of the many point-to-point meetings or already on a racecourse, a future star is tuning up ready to put the Irish horse back in his customary position, at the forefront of the equestrian world.

Fatalities are an unfortunate part of jump racing, but are usually swiftly dealt with by the Blue Cross horse ambulance.

CHAPTER SEVEN

HUNTING

A BRACE OF Germans viewed, with unconcealed and increasing horror, the mayhem in front of them as half the mounted field plummetted into the ravening maws that precede the famous double banks in the Golden Vale of Tipperary. 'This isn't hunting, this is Vietnam!' one of them uttered, as yet another equine form and its human partner were swallowed up by the yawning chasms.

Such tales may deter the fainthearted. Or they may, as in the case of a Dublin journalist about to make his debut on the hunting field after forty years of the sedentary life, cause wills to be drawn up and witnessed by members of the hunting party before hounds move off. But for the true hunting enthusiast there is nowhere in the world that offers more varied or more challenging country to cross in pursuit of the fox, the hare or the stag than Ireland.

Co. Galway is described as a huntsman's paradise because of its unrivalled characteristic that the huntsman can always see his hounds in front of him and the mounted field is constantly in touch with the pack. It is unusual for even the stragglers to get lost in this flat landscape, which is probably a good thing as the light limestone soil barely reflects the passing of sixty or seventy horses and hoofprints cannot be relied upon to trail the passage of the hunt. It is undoubtedly the ideal surface for falling on should your horse fail to negotiate one of the stone walls successfully. The cleaning bill will not be greatly increased, but you are almost certain to land on a stone, and if you don't, your horse definitely will.

The chief pack in the county, the Galway Blazers reputedly earned their name following a visit to the neighbouring Ormond hunt which ended, naturally enough, in the local hostelry, Dooley's Hotel, in Birr, Co. Offaly. The resulting revelry got rather out of hand, however, and Dooley's became the victim, perishing in the flames of its own funeral pyre. There is also a theory put forward that two of the Galway committee members, D'Arcy and Burke, were possessed of flaming red hair, but it is the former argument that carries more weight.

Stone walls, literally hundreds of them, are the feature of Galway, while Limerick, Tipperary and Cork offer the delights of the huge double banks, with drains fore and aft. In Wexford the banks are narrow, razor-topped singles, often with a ditch on the landing side to catch out the over-

OPPOSITE: Raymond Keogh, former joint-Master of the Ward Union Staghounds. ABOVE: The staghounds in action.

exuberant horse who tries to fly the whole lot in one go. And then there are the infamous drains of Co. Meath, vast valleys which can comfortably accommodate horses, and frequently riders as well, should they fail to make the far bank.

In previous years the Meath mounted field would attract its familiar teams of wreckers who would always be on hand to assist. These were groups of the more solidly built males of the area, equipped with ropes and spades which would be wielded only on the production of a suitable sum of money. A breakdown in negotiations whilst fixing the price would merely leave the horse floundering around in the bottom of the drain and eventually the exasperated horseman would relent and pay up. It was not unknown for the wreckers to actually encourage visitors to tackle a particularly treacherous obstacle in order to boost the day's takings and, if this ploy failed to pay dividends, a helping hand back into the ditch as the unfortunate animal teetered on the brink usually brought about the required result.

The hunting world has always been well endowed with characters. Probably one of the best known in Ireland is Lady Mollie Cusack-Smith, Master of the Galway Blazers for four

seasons at the start of the Second World War before she and her husband Sir Dermot founded the Bermingham and North Galway in 1946. Lady Mollie was to carry the horn for thirty-eight years with her own pack.

Lady Mollie's language in the hunting field was legendary, as was the sport she showed with the pack. Her hunt ball remains one of the few social fixtures that still reflects the glory of the old days when Dublin Horse Show week required powers of endurance beyond the call of duty and the dancing went on all night every night. It is not just dancing that continues on into the small hours at Bermingham House. Lady Mollie recalls finding the lawn strewed with hunt buttons one post-ball morning after an argument had degenerated into a fist fight. Unfortunately one of the pugilists failed to realize that he was taking on a prize fighter and was lucky to lose only his buttons in the ensuing mêlée.

Mollie O'Rourke's hunting days are over now, but she still claims to love dancing better than anything. Friends say she was eighty-three at the beginning of the 1990s, but Lady Mollie, affronted at being asked, claims she is most definitely 102. She also states that she cannot remember when she gave

RIGHT AND OPPOSITE: Hunt balls are still all about dressing up, even though a wide variety of dress lengths will be on display. Black tie, mess uniform and the hunt evening dress all rub shoulders with the glamour of the ladies and, in a setting as glorious as Bermingham House, scene of the Bermingham and North Galway hunt ball for many years, it is definitely worth the effort. Lady Mollie Cusack-Smith (CENTRE) toasts her guests at Bermingham House, in front of a painting of John Dennis, founder of the Galway Blazers.

up hunting hounds. 'Maths was never my strong point. I got 2 out of 100 for arithmetic at school. They said they gave me 2 for trying, but I didn't try at all!'

She was not any good at blowing the hunting horn either when she first started. But, having been described by an uncle as a jack of all trades and master of none, she decided that she should become a Master of Foxhounds, for which blowing the horn was an undeniable prerequisite if she was to hunt hounds herself. So she persevered 'at Ascot and at nightclubs' until she eventually drew the first note out of the reluctant instrument at her house near Grosvenor Square in London to which she had retreated when her father continued to press her into the one thing in life she hated almost as much as maths, riding horses. On hearing the unusual sound of a hunting horn in the middle of London, a girlfriend living on the other side of the square instantly rang Mollie to congratulate her on her achievement. By the time she returned to Ireland the trained opera singer and dressmaker had added a new skill to her repertoire and was to become renowned for her music on the horn through which she communicated with her hounds.

In spite of the fact that hunting was her life for well over forty years, she says she never liked horses. They were a conveyance, a means of getting from one covert side to another and the only way to keep in touch with her beloved hounds. She reminisces about her favourite hound, Planter. He had been branded a rogue by the Co. Galway huntsman even as a youngster, before he had been entered into that prodigious hunting force. 'He was an absolutely brilliant unentered hound. He'd had blazing rows with the new whip who said he was dangerous. I was unentered too, so I took him and he became the foundation sire of my whole pack.' Planter was later loaned to the neighbouring Westmeath as a stallion hound. One of his descendants is now back with the Bermingham and North Galway and quickly became one of huntsman John Pickering's favourites. Godfrey possesses the same abundant personality that characterized his grandfather and, if a meet is cancelled, displays his fury by sitting in the hound trailer, howling and refusing to be tempted back into kennels.

Hunting continued in wartime Ireland, unhindered by the threat of bombs which had closed down sport in England. It

John Pickering, a true
professional in the art of hunting
hounds, can show a surprising
turn of foot across the most
difficult country if hounds are
running.

was during the war, while Mollie was hunting the Galway Blazers, that she and her second whipper-in found themselves alone with hounds after a terrific run. Miles from anywhere, they hacked their steaming horses to the first pub they could find. Hounds were watered and horses Guinnessed, while Lady Mollie quenched her thirst with a pint of cider topped up with a large brandy. The moon was already up by the time they embarked on the 17-mile journey to Bermingham House, where hounds were camping while hunting the Tuam side of the country. The town clock was just striking midnight as the weary travellers and their pack clattered into Tuam, causing terror amongst the locals who thought it was a ghostly visitation from Black Jack, alias John Dennis, the original Master of the Co. Galway hounds back in 1839.

Lady Mollie was to be responsible for introducing one of the county's most famous sons to hunting. Lord Hemphill, Senior Steward of the Turf Club from 1985 to 1988, was to be Master of the Blazers for twenty-nine years. But he made his first entrance into the sport as an eight-year-old boy, who had been dispatched down to Bermingham House on strict instructions not to go hunting. 'So we did. Immediately,' says Lady Mollie with glee. 'The only trouble was that his mother

had bought him a hat that was much too big for him. She said that he'd grow into it! Either the hat or Peter Patrick fell off at every single fence.' Lord Hemphill remembers the day clearly too. But he also looks back with unconcealed pride on what his predecessor at the head of the field claims was the best hunt in Galway since 1906.

After an almost completely blank day Lady Mollie's hounds found just after three o'clock and, on a screaming scent, ran from Castlehacket to Anaghadown, a distance of 9 miles, but 21 miles as hounds ran. The pack was pursuing its quarry straight into the setting sun, leaving the field to follow virtually blind and unable to see what they were jumping or who was still in touch. Well up at the front, but already showing some wear and tear, was Lord Hemphill who was riding his wife Ann's mare Billie Jean as his own horse had been injured and taken back to the box by Lady Hemphill. Aware that the mare was not really up to his weight and aware too that the pace was beginning to ask some rather searching questions of his own fitness, Lord Hemphill was not sorry when he jumped out onto a road straight in front of his own car. Tumbling off the mare he called to his wife to take over in the saddle, a request which was obeyed without

147

demur and the new combination vanished into the dusk. By the time hounds put their fox to ground it was pitch dark, but of the seven finishers, four were recognizable as Hemphills, including young Charles riding the three-year-old Connemara pony colt Tulira Rocket on his first day's hunting.

The hunting priest is by no means a creation of Surtees or the Victorian novelist. One of the most popular figures in the

The Blazers pack in full cry after their quarry.

Blazers' field was Father Loughnane, who was never known to miss his Tuesday out with the Galway pack, even though his parish was in Quin, Co. Clare. He did make one concession to his calling, however, resisting the temptation to hunt on Saturdays so that he could take confession. His bishop was driven to distraction as he vainly urged the priest to think more of God than of the fox. Father Loughnane's parishioners were well used to seeing a well-polished hunting boot sticking out from under his surplice and even believed his vestments were lined with fox fur. But it was felt that even he had gone too far when his always late return from the Galway Tuesday meet was delayed yet further and he ended up joining the funeral cortège, horse box in tow, and proceeded to take the funeral service in full hunting regalia.

For this misdemeanour he was banished to Loop Head, the westernmost point of Co. Clare, in the hope that the distance at least would dampen the errant priest's enthusiasm for the chase. But Father Loughnane promptly started his own private pack to keep himself amused and, instead of towing

his horse to Galway for his Tuesday visits, simply bought a faster car and installed his mount in a livery yard.

His death in 1987 was a sad loss and hunt members still recall the day when Lady Ampthill, riding side-saddle as usual, disappeared into a ditch only to be totally ignored by the normally gallant Father Loughnane. Quizzed afterwards as to why he had not made any attempt to help the lady in distress, the good Father reasoned simply, 'What with hounds running? You surely couldn't expect me to stop. Unless of course she was in need of spiritual attention!'

But Father Loughnane was not alone in living and breathing hunting. Lady Hemphill, founder of the internationally famous Connemara pony stud at Tulira Castle, resisted the lures of the chase on only one day of the week during more than four decades in the saddle. A direct descendant of Robert Parsons Persse, whose Castleboy hunt was the forerunner of the Blazers (later to be hunted for thirty-three seasons by Burton Persse), Lady Hemphill was recognized as one of the finest women to hounds in the world. Her near constant absence from the home prompted the children's nanny to remark to her youthful charges, 'We might see more of your mother if we had four legs in the nursery.'

Galway is dismissed by the uninitiated as easy country to cross. But the rider needs an accurate eye if his horse is to survive jumping well in excess of 100 walls in a day without some damage to his knees. The walls are very upright, with no ditches or undergrowth in front to make a horse stand off his fences. The steel-hearted P. P. Hogan, who would tackle the most terrifying obstacles anywhere else, hates the very sight of stone walls. Stricken with what appeared to be acute appendicitis, he was rushed to hospital by Ann Hemphill and the brilliant Morny Wing, the jockey that realized Vincent O'Brien's famous 1944 autumn double with Drybob and Good Days. As the car scorched along the twisty, narrow lanes in its mercy dash, the recumbent figure on the back seat suddenly ceased its groaning and sat up. But the sight of a large wall at Herbertstown was enough to pitch it back into the horizontal plane, exclaiming in the process, 'I'd even prefer to be jumping that than going where you're taking me'.

There is a saving grace for the wall hater in Galway, however. If a particularly large obstacle looms into view, the wallophobe needs only to remain with the similarly minded at the back of the field and there will be little left for him to jump. In the wake of the demolition gang come two full-time workers, employed by the hunt to resurrect the walls after the less able members of the field have left a trail of destruction in their wake.

But the Blazers' followers do occasionally meet rather more hazardous obstacles, such as the Claregalway river in spate. Lancelot Smith, a steward at the RDS and Master of the Blazers between 1952 and 1956, attempted to cross the swollen waters after the fox and its pursuing pack had managed to negotiate the swirling torrents. Master and horse were instantly swept downstream, the horse eventually being beached on a small area of bank that had survived the floods. In desperation, Lance Smith grabbed an overhanging branch and was clinging on, literally, with his teeth. While the rest of the field looked on in impotent horror, Bill King, a famous submarine commander, threw off his hunting coat and dived in, boots and all, to go to the rescue. Without a thought for his own safety he managed to achieve his objective and brought the wretched and half-drowned Smith out on the far side of the river. The exhausted horse had meanwhile managed to scramble to its feet and, pausing only briefly to proffer his thanks to his saviour, Lance Smith swung himself back into the saddle and went on another 3 miles to kill his fox. With the adrenalin suddenly drained from his system he then collapsed.

Another character who refuses to be ignored in Blazers country is Willie Leahy, who followed in the footsteps of Lady Hemphill as fieldmaster for this popular pack which attracts a huge number of visitors. Willie encourages these welcome additions to the field as he is the chief provider of the hirelings on which they enjoy their day's sport. At least two Leahy lorries, one or both of which will also be towing a trailer, arrive at each meet and horses tumble apparently unceasingly from their dark recesses. None are tied for the journeys, but are loaded in herringbone fashion, with a heavyweight saved till last to give that extra shove to squeeze in another body.

One visitor, suitably mounted on a Leahy hireling, managed to part company with his horse in the course of the day's action. Voices enquired if he was all right as their owners sailed over his head. Yes, he replied, he was fine. Obviously not quite as fine as he had initially diagnosed, he came to some considerable time later. Darkness was descending rapidly. Hounds, horses and humans had left no trace of their passing. Unfamiliar with the surrounding countryside, the visitor did not even know which way to aim in order to reach the nearest road. Striking out across the sheep-grazed Galway turf, the lost soul eventually found his way to a road after a not inconsiderable hike which involved scaling the crumbling stone walls that constantly crossed his path and which he had so delighted in jumping earlier that day.

Hailing the first car that came towards him, he enquired how far he was from the meet. 'Oh, about 8 miles,' said a female voice gaily. 'Sorry, can't stop. Late for a dinner party,' shouted the driver as she sped off again in a cloud of dust and exhaust fumes. The occupant of the next vehicle took pity on our reluctant traveller, however, bringing him back to the meet where he had to face Willie Leahy and explain the loss of his horse, painfully aware that he had also booked another

Although Blazers country is typified by the criss-cross pattern of stone walls, the southernmost part of the hunt country below Loughrea is much rougher, with thicker cover and greater foliage on the walls that do occasionally appear.

mount for the following day. He did not expect to meet with a favourable response.

'Here, hold this one,' said Willie, handing a headcollar rope to the new arrival, as he went through the complicated manoeuvres necessary to wedge yet another trusty steed into the lorry. 'Where's yours?' he then enquired as he became aware that the newcomer had returned by means of rather different horsepower to the one on which he had left that morning. He was not in the least bit perturbed when he heard that the horse had gone awol and there was never any question of missing the next day's hunting because of the incident. The only problem, as far as Willie could see, was that the four-legged absentee was still wearing the visitor's saddle. The poor beast was eventually found at three o'clock the following afternoon, grazing quite happily. The saddle and its wearer were perfectly unharmed, probably delighted to have been awarded an unexpected day's holiday.

Falls are an accepted part of hunting and most wound the

pride more than the person. Unfortunately the light soil of Galway does not extend to the rest of the country and fallers are instantly recognizable due to the layer of mud that liberally adorns part, or all, of their clothing. But few fallers have emerged quite so well coated with this more substantial of the elements than a visiting Swiss journalist on one of his annual forays to hunt in Ireland. The day in question involved a lawn meet of the Co. Limerick foxhounds at Bobby Barry's Mellon Stud, home of some of the finest bloodstock in the country.

The yard that was providing the scribe with his mount for the day had been forewarned that this particular jockey was exceedingly tall and had therefore provided a suitably tall horse. But the stirrup leathers failed to match up to the height of either the horse or the rider. A search for a new pair was instituted, but hounds had already moved off, the field obediently hacking along the side of a dugout drain of quite horrifying dimensions. Its width decreased further up the field, however, and the followers negotiated the obstacle without too much drama before hacking back down the other side.

The Swiss visitor meanwhile, equipped with the necessary attachments on his saddle to accommodate his lengthy limbs, emerged through the gate and, seeing his colleagues on the far side of the drain, rashly launched his horse and himself over the divide. Without the benefit of a warm-up and pointed at the widest part of the ditch, the unfortunate pair pitched headlong into the depths of liquid mud at the bottom. The hours spent that morning grooming both the equine and human form to perfection were destroyed in an instant and the pair had to suffer the indignity of wearing this incriminating extra layer throughout the day, even their teeth bearing witness to the slimy immersion.

Another Swiss visitor, who had been told bloodchilling stories over dinner about an even worse obstacle which had to be negotiated at the following day's meet, feared a similar fate. One of the Co. Limerick foxhounds' most famous coverts is at Dromin. But its fame partly revolves around the awesome dimensions of the drain known in the district as the Black Trench. The double bank which this main sewer from the local creamery encloses is unavoidable if hounds run in a southerly direction.

The dinner party for the Swiss ambassador proved a great success, not least because the hostess' plans for a Grand Marnier soufflé went by the board when she discovered the house to be totally devoid of the required spirit. Poitín was used in its place, a substitute with which the guests became rapidly enamoured and their tales about the Black Trench

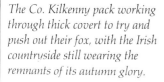

The Co. Kilkenny pack working through thick covert to try and push out their fox, with the Irish countryside still wearing the remnants of its autumn glory.

were embellished in direct proportion to the helpings of soufflé consumed.

Resigning himself to stinking humiliation at best and drowning at worst, the Swiss ambassador mounted his horse the following morning sickeningly aware of the inevitability of it all. The opening followed the prescribed path, and hounds, finding almost immediately, ran straight towards the dreaded trench. But the poitín was made of sterner stuff than the ambassador and, when hounds checked four fields later, the wielder of army knives was again nearly speechless, this time with delight at having undergone this trial by trench and made it to the other side. But his celebrations were cut short when the huntsman and hounds, having cast in vain for the line, retraced their steps in order to draw the covert again. This certainly was not cricket, thought the outraged ambassador to himself. Nobody had mentioned the fact that he might have to jump the nightmare drain twice in the same day!

One faller who escaped the indignity of a mudbath but nearly lost his head in the process was the jockey Jimmy Doyle, who was one of many out with the now disbanded Naas Harriers that had imbibed fairly liberally at the hunt ball the night before. The Harriers were kennelled at the Curragh Camp and it was traditional that the action on the day after

the ball was a drag laid from the camp right across the Curragh to the Red Hills. Keen to get to the front lines, Doyle put his head down and set off at a flat out gallop, only to be dramatically halted in his flight and hauled bodily from his horse as he collided with a clothes line. Thankfully Doyle's horse that day was a fairly sizeable one and the rope caught his jockey in the chest.

Ireland has two packs of staghounds, the Co. Down in northern Ireland and the Ward Union which are kennelled at Ashbourne in Co. Meath. The Wards are particularly popular and attract more than their share of the hard-riding, well-heeled set, who have earned themselves the sobriquet, the Grafton Street Harriers.

But the pace of the staghunt requires a good horse and, above all, supreme horsemanship to survive the rigours of a very testing country. According to Standish Collen, Master of the Ward Union from 1962 to 1967, a good stag can wear out a good pack of hounds, good men and good horses. But it is the outliers, stags which have managed to elude the pursuing pack and evade capture, that provide some of the most memorable hunts. The taste of freedom, however brief, seems to instil into the outlier a wiliness more usually associated with the fox.

Standish Collen remembers vividly a five-hour hunt after an outlier which ended in the encroaching darkness at a small cottage out in the depths of Ward Union country. A fire was

ABOVE: Wall jumping is an accomplishment, but not all mounted followers achieve or aspire to any great degree of proficiency. As long as horse and rider get over the obstacle without permanent separation, the results are satisfactory, to the rider at least.

LEFT: The terrierman, here Gill Morrissey of the Blazers, still has an important role to play in the day-to-day work of a hunt if the pack's foremost reason for existence, that of controlling foxes, is to be safeguarded.

151

blazing in the hearth and the grandmother was toasting her toes from the capacious depths of an armchair next to it. On the far side of the fireplace a cot contained a child wrapped in the sleep of the innocent, while its mother put the finishing touches to the evening meal before the men came in for their tea. As she reached up to take the plates down from a dresser well furnished with crockery, the door burst open and the stag, having seen this haven from afar, careered into the room.

The combined forces of the late Jim Ryan, Charlie McCann and Standish Collen had managed to restrain the pack from joining its quarry at the hearth, but the human trio had determined that they were going to catch this one, whatever the consequences. Minus the canine element the chase continued round the kitchen table and the stag finally gave in to the huntsman, allowing himself to be returned to the cart from which he had made good his escape so many weeks earlier. And, although the baby was roused from its slumber and granny shaken from her reverie, not so much as an egg-cup was cracked in the taking of this determined outlier.

But there is an epilogue to the story. About ten years later hounds were hunting in the same area and Standish Collen had stopped to pay his respects to a farmer who was holding a gate open for the field. 'Time has been good to you,' said the man. 'You're looking well.' Standish offered a polite but noncommittal reply, unaware of ever having seen the man before. 'Well don't you recognize herself?,' continued the farmer, indicating the ruddy-cheeked, auburn-haired girl that clung to his hand. 'This is the wee one that was in the cot that night when you came to collect your deer.'

The Ward Union claims to be one of the oldest staghound packs in Europe, dating back to 1828 when two separate packs, the Dubber and the Hollywood, hunted the present Ward Union country. By 1830 the two packs had been amalgamated to form the Wards, but it was not until 1854 that the full title of Ward Union Staghounds was used when the Wards joined forces with Mr Broadley's Staghounds, which Lord Howth had brought over from Leamington fourteen years earlier.

The northern staghound pack, the Co. Down, was established in 1881. Previously a harrier pack, it had originally been hunted by Captain R. B. Ker. The switch to red deer came about in 1881 and stag has been the quarry ever since over this enormously varied country in which fences of all types are met.

George Bryson, Master of the Co. Down from 1971 to 1980 and one of the founders of eventing in northern Ireland, would spend a considerable amount of time schooling his horses for the rigour of the chase over his own and his neighbour's land. That neighbour was Bill Buller, an Olympic horse trials rider who went on to become president of the Equestrian Federation of Ireland. His Scarvagh House estate

was the venue for northern Ireland's first three-day event, giving both Buller and Bryson plenty of material for schooling sessions.

Following in his neighbour's wake, George Bryson had tried to put his horse over wire three times. Each attempt had met with the same result, the horse turned cartwheels over the fence. As the object of the session was to teach the horse to jump, not to fall, the pair hacked on to a drain to continue the lesson. The effect was similar here except that Bryson's horse, having finally learnt something, tried out a new routine by jamming on the brakes. But he had not even grasped the rudiments of stopping by this stage and, making his decision

too late, slid into the bottom of the ditch, decanting Bryson over his head.

Terminating the lesson there and then, Bryson scrambled out of the ditch and, without a backward glance at his erstwhile partner, started striding out across the field, much to the consternation of Buller who inquired whether his friend was suffering from concussion. 'No,' replied Bryson, 'I'm going home for my tea.'

Bryson was highly revered in the hunting field, however, commanding the respect of his followers through quiet discipline. Misdemeanours were rewarded with banishment from the rest of the day's sport and culprits were all dealt with

equally including, on one occasion, his own daughter.

The local farmers also had great respect for Bryson, whose horsemanship always gave him the edge across the country. As Master and hounds hove into view during one hunt, a landowner, knowing that no obstacle would prevent Bryson from keeping in touch with the pack, was heard to say to his child, 'You may open the gate son. You might as well try and stop the Queen as stop him coming through.'

Standish Collen, loyal to his own southern staghound pack, claims to have had all his best sport with the Ward Union. But he has seen action with packs all over England and Ireland. Before the death of his wife Claire, Standish made annual trips

This hunters' moon may not dispense the liquid refreshment available in the Ashbourne hostelry of the same name, where the Ward Union Staghounds hold their St Stephen's Day meet, but its appearance signalled the beginning of the end of their day's hunting.

National Hunt trainer Mouse Morris is fearless across the big bank country of Tipperary.

down to Limerick, stabling six horses at the Dunraven Arms Hotel in Adare, from where Claire, Mr Collen senior and he would hunt with the Black and Tans, the Co. Limerick and the United as well as the Limerick Harriers under the late Peg Watt.

A feature of those Limerick visits was the rivalry between Standish and Pat Hogan, a not unfamiliar name in the horse world. The pair were, like their present-day counterparts Timmy Hyde and Mouse Morris, notoriously hard riders across the country, both doing their level best to upend the other one in the process.

Standish was lucky enough to have a brilliant point-to-pointer to hunt, giving him that comforting awareness that he could tackle the biggest country without qualms. Skyhooks had won nine of his eleven starts in the point-to-point field, being beaten in the other two by a neck and a head having fallen and been remounted by Standish.

A day out with Peg Watt's Limerick Harriers always offered what Standish refers to as 'a mixed grill' of hunting the fox, the hare or a drag. On the day in question it was widely known that the final run would be a drag. It was also widely known that Pat Hogan had laid it. 'There was a tightening of girths and shortening of leathers,' recounts Standish. 'The tension was mounting and I knew that the drag was imminent.'

As is always the case with drag hunting, hounds flew off at a breakneck pace, the field plunging after them *en masse*. But, having been surrounded by fellow followers one moment, Standish was disconcerted to realize that he was suddenly on his own with hounds directly in front of him. At some stage the field had veered off in the opposite direction, leaving Standish, as he realized afterwards, to his fate.

But it was not long before the cause of this mass exodus was revealed. A huge ravine of a ditch opened up in front of Standish and Skyhooks. Even by Meath standards this was a big one. As he peered down into its depths Standish was galvanized into action with the thought that if P.P. could jump it so could he. Taking Skyhooks back to get a good run at it, Standish faced the horse at the embryonic valley whose ghastly dimensions were made even more appalling by the fact that the landing was considerably higher than the take-off. Skyhooks took it in his stride. But what neither he nor his rider knew was that P.P. had not even attempted to jump this monstrosity. He had laid the drag by foot up to that point and then joined forces with his horse which had been patiently awaiting his arrival, tethered on the far side of the ditch.

Big open drains are also a feature of Laois, where the county pack enjoys the reputation of tough country that requires a true hunter to survive both the ditches and banks that are met in a day's hunting. Dessie Lalor, Master of the Co. Laois foxhounds from 1964 to 1978, is proud of this

notoriety, rising to the challenge of these big fences well into his seventies. An offer to take over the horn with the neighbouring Ormonds early in his hunting career was turned down, in spite of the fact that Dessie regards the Ormond country as 'very lovable' with its fly fences and the odd bank and ditch.

The Laois was formerly known as the Queens County which traces back, through several private packs, to 1778 when John Barrington kept hounds at Knapton in Abbeyleix.

Dessie Lalor's retirement in 1978 was widely regretted. His final hunt as Master was from Ballyfin on 29 March and, as hounds were stopped close to six that evening and the field prepared to hack down the mountainside back to the meet, a rainbow decked the heavens in a final tribute to the retiring Master.

His friend over the years, Jack Murphy, is still at the helm with the nearby North Kilkennys. The pack dates back only as far as 1934 and Murphy came in as Master seven years later, to become one of the longest serving masters in the country.

Two of Co. Cork's foxhound packs, the Muskerry and Duhallow, officially date back to the middle of the eighteenth century, but there are much earlier records of hunting in Ireland. King Brian Boru, vanquisher of the Danes at the Battle of Clontarf in 1059, reputedly hunted with his own pack of hounds.

There have been other equally famous Masters whose reputations have been earned on the hunting rather than the battlefield. In the opinions of many, however, including the two Germans mentioned at the beginning of this chapter, it is debatable whether there is any notable difference between the two.

The name of John Watson is still probably the best known in Irish hunting circles. Master of the Meaths between 1891 and 1908, Watson bred what was acknowledged at the time as being the most perfect pack of hounds in Ireland and possibly the world. He kept three packs of hounds in kennels and hunted five days a week, saving the sixth for a spin with the neighbouring Ward Union. The Meaths' Tuesday and Friday meets in Co. Dublin country attracted fields of nearly 500 and Watson himself would refer to these fixtures as the battlefields.

During the cubhunting season Watson would be out at the crack of dawn with his hounds and would then spend the rest of the day playing polo in the Phoenix Park until darkness put a stop to his sport. But it was his heart that finally cut short this frenetic pace and, having returned the mastership of the Meaths to his predecessor Lord Fingall, the 56-year-old Watson died shortly afterwards.

Carrying the Meath horn now is Johnny Henry who took over the pack in 1956 as the youngest huntsman in Ireland or England. His brilliance with hounds and the superb sport he

Michael Higgens, Master and huntsman of the four-day-a-week Co. Tipperary foxhounds, retired at the end of the 1990/91 season after seventeen years hunting hounds. In the background are the medieval walls of Fethard.

shows with the bitch pack have caused his name to be spoken of in tandem with John Watson's and, in Meath country anyway, he is considered the best huntsman since his famous forerunner.

Ikey (Isaac) Bell is another respected name in the annals of Irish hunting history. Master of the Blazers from 1903 to 1908, Bell, like so many great men, was only awarded the recognition he deserved after he had retired. While cubhunting one morning in the far reaches of the Blazers' country, he was provided with some invaluable assistance from the local old stagers, all of whom claimed to have been blooded by Burton Persse who had hunted hounds during the first half of the nineteenth century. Following a successful conclusion to the morning's endeavours, Bell went round and individually thanked all the old retainers who had been involved. It was one of their number who remarked in indulgent tones that, if Bell persevered at his trade, he might one day be as good a huntsman as old Burton.

Lord Daresbury, a former Master of the Belvoir between 1943 and 1947, is another name that ranks with the all-time greats. He took over the Co. Limerick foxhounds on his retirement from the Belvoir and was to remain at the helm for thirty years, only taking on a joint-Master to share the responsibilities in 1970.

While still ruling singlehandedly, this much revered Master was introduced to what must have ranked as an abomination in his eyes, used to seeing both his field and his own person immaculately turned out for the day's sport. The apparition was none other than Charles Douglas-Hume, nephew of the then British Prime Minister, Sir Alec Douglas-Hume. The Beatles had just sprung to fame and had brought with them a fashion that was to outlive even their apparently undying popularity. But while long hair was accepted and expected in London society, it looked more than a little out of place in the hunting field of Ireland's most respected pack. Especially as its wearer was also decked out in a pre-First World War hunting coat that, either due to age or the strange proclivities of its former owner, was an odd yellow hue. Completing the ensemble was an excessively battered top hat.

The strangely attired figure was a guest of Alan and Lady Vivienne Lillingston, neither of whom was relishing having to do the honours and introduce their companion to the Master. It was Vivi who eventually summoned up the necessary reserves of courage, presenting the newcomer to Lord Daresbury before he had been given time to contemplate sending him home. After all the usual pleasantries had been gone through, the mortified hostess then mumbled her apologies for her guest's unorthodox dress code. 'Not at all, don't worry about it,' said Lord Daresbury. 'If the fox sees him we'll have a 10-mile point at least!'

The neighbouring pack to the Co. Limerick is possibly the best known outside Ireland and certainly one of the best loved inside the country. The Scarteen hounds, universally called the Black and Tans because of its unique pack which traces back to the Kerry beagle, have been in the Ryan family for over 300 years. An extract from the family papers, dated 1691 after the Battle of Aughrim and the Treaty of Limerick, refer to 'O'Mulrian, on an earlier date before the Cromwellian confiscations, gave up Jacobite soldiering and took to farming and hunting and, since those days, have been farming and hunting through thick and thin.' The family papers also record the opening of new kennels at Scarteen in an entry dated 8 September, 1904. 'Hounds came over from Emly. They went there in 1890. Uncle Clem, Jack and Clem walked them over the fields ... 13 dogs and 17 bitches, 15 couple in all.'

It was in 1904 that John J. Ryan, father of the world famous Thady Ryan, took over the pack, following in the footsteps of generations of Ryans. The family pack seemed destined to lose its new Master ten years later, however, when John Ryan

joined the 16th Lancers on the outbreak of the First World War.

The ghastly but not unexpected news filtered back to Limerick that Ryan and his company had been blown up and buried in a trench and all were officially listed as dead. A fund was immediately started to erect a memorial to the late Master in the local village of Emly. But the Ryans are made of tougher stuff than that and John Ryan was dug out alive by a high-ranking German officer who, incredibly, recognized him having hunted with the Scarteens before the war, riding one of Ryan's horses. Although capture was inevitable, John Ryan was accorded special privileges throughout his enforced stay in Germany.

It was several months before the glad tidings reached Emly, at which point the plans for the memorial were abandoned and the funds were diverted into the coffers of the nearest whiskey retailers to provide the chief requirement for a massive celebration.

Fox and hare were the chief quarry at the turn of the century, but when foxes became scarce, forays were made to local woods or even as far afield as Loughcutra in Co. Galway to capture stags which were then reared at the Scarteen kennels. It was not until 1928 that an end was put to the pack's staghunting, although the older members of the family still look back on those days with a certain fondness.

Gwenda Pearson, sister of Thady Ryan and secretary to the Black and Tans, recalls the deer park at Scarteen. 'It was really only a paddock and the terriers were constantly breaking in and chasing the deer for hours before we could catch them. Our father used to tell us not to bother as it would keep the deer fit for hunting.'

John Ryan returned to the fold at the end of the war to take up the Scarteen horn once more. He remained as sole Master of the pack until 1946 when he was joined by his son Thady, eventually retiring eleven years later to leave hounds in Thady's more than capable hands.

Thady was a mere twenty-three when he joined his father in the mastership, but he had already had experience of hunting hounds. During the Second World War John Ryan was struck down by a particularly virulent strain of pneumonia and retired to his bed. Thady was called upon to abandon his role as Master of the Ampleforth College beagles and return to hunt the family pack. Thady and his two sisters, Gwenda and Jean, who were at that time whipping-in to their father, drove the fourteen miles to the meet in a pony and trap. All three were in a state of nervous apprehension about the task that awaited Thady, but were well enough to consume their entire day's rations *en route*.

During his forty-one seasons as Master of the Scarteens, Thady Ryan earned a reputation for providing unbeatable sport over the huge double banks of the country. The striking

Michael Dempsey, joint-Master and huntsman of the Galway Blazers.

black and tan hounds, which uniquely possess a hare foot rather than the cat foot of the foxhound, have the most wonderful voice, which would lift the heart of even the city dweller who has never had the joy of following a pack in full cry over some of the best country in Ireland.

Thady knew and loved every individual hound and their devotion to him was obvious when he paraded the pack at Dublin Horse Show one year. After galloping around the ring with hounds streaming after him, Thady then jumped up onto the bank at the top end of the arena. Every single hound obediently and unhesitatingly followed its master onto the bank, a never to be forgotten sight and one which is unlikely ever to be repeated.

A deeply religious man, it was Thady who instituted the blessing of hounds, followers and landowners at the opening meet in Knocklong. This has now become an ecumenical blessing performed by the local Church of Ireland minister and the parish priest, and is one of the rituals that highlights the start of the new hunting season. In recent years nobody can remember the blessing taking place in anything other than a downpour.

Regardless of the weather, the blessing is always held, even though it is now without its creator. Thady emigrated to New Zealand in April 1987 to allow his wife Anne to return to the country of her birth. The couple took with them an Irish Draught stallion, Kingsway Diamond, by King of Diamonds, and two fillies in the hope of using these as the foundation stock for crossing with the tough New Zealand-bred horses. The experiment is proving a success and Thady, always an ambassador for Ireland and particularly the Irish horse, is continuing to promote the bloodlines that for so many years carried him with such agility in the hunting field.

He is sorely missed in Ireland. His departure is almost worse than his death as his friends at home reflect on the fact that others are now benefitting from his genius while Ireland suffers from the loss of it. Thankfully the Black and Tans live on and remain in the Ryan family, continuing to provide the level of sport that was Thady's hallmark, even though he, with his customary generosity, gave all the credit to his hounds. His son Chris has taken over the horn and, while lacking Thady's depth of knowledge, is already showing flashes of the genius that marked out Thady from the rest of the pack.

Thady Ryan and the other great Masters over the years have epitomized all that is best in Irish hunting. They are the catalysts that bring together the hounds, the unique Irish countryside and, most important of all, the Irish horse to produce hunting that is, quite simply, beyond compare.

Jerome Mahony, Chairman of the Blazers.

GENERAL INDEX

INDEX OF HORSES